GRANDFATHER PARKYN'S ECLIPSE

A diary written on a journey from Par, Cornwall to Edinburgh in July 1927 taking in the Eclipse in its Totality in Richmond, Yorkshire.

Editor Joy David

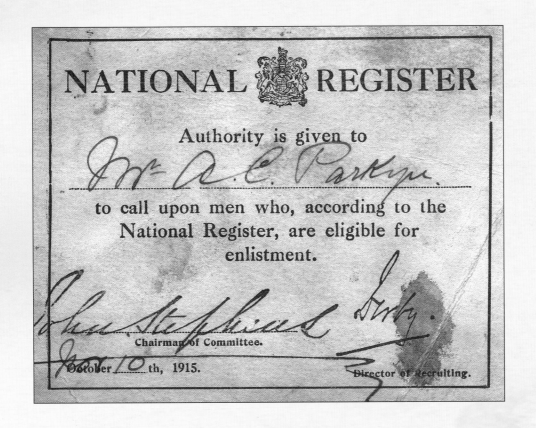

Grandfathers Parkyn's Eclipse
Acknowledgment

Joy David has had so much enthusiastic help from people in getting Grandfather Parkyn's Eclipse ready for publication saying thank you individually has become impossible. However, there are some people who have exceeded the call of duty! Bridget Williams & David Stephens of Sainsbury's archive department, Freda Cooper of Sainsbury's, Alan Cameron of the Fiat Register, The Fiat Motor Club of Great Britain and my colleagues Mick Devereux and Jamie Macleod all deserve especial thanks. Finally we are all indebted to The Motor Museum at Beaulieu for their assistance in setting up the charming front cover. Nor should we forget Trevor Parkyn George who has secreted Grandfather Parkyn's diary for many years before he fortuitously told me about it over lunch one Sunday. We are indebted to Sainsbury's & Beaulieu Motor Museum for the front cover picture.

ISBN 1 899311 65 3
First published 1999
Copyright Joy David
All rights reserved

British Library Catalogue-In-Publication Data
Catalogue Data is available from the British Library

Published by JDC Publications, 138 Alexandra Road, Plymouth PL2 1JY
Tel: 01752 605997 E-mail joy@travellerschoice.net
Printed and bound in Great Britain by Picture House Press
14 Tamar View Industrial Estate, Saltash, Cornwall PL12 6LD

DISTRIBUTION BY: ABA Book Distribution. FREEPOST (PY2100). Plymouth PL2 1BF
Telephone 01752 559999   Fax 01752 558888

ALFRED CHARLES PARKYN
1863-1950
From Trevor Parkyn George

My Grandfather Alfred Charles Parkyn was born in 1863 in Par, Cornwall. The eldest of three children he had a brother and sister. He left school at the age of 11 years and worked with his father John Parkyn who had a Ship's Chandlery and Grocery business. John Parkyn also owned property in Par consisting of his own house and shop and about 13 cottages which were rented to the working families of the area. On his death Alfred Charles Parkyn, my Grandfather, inherited the business he had worked in from a boy into adult life.

His sister received the house and a small legacy; the remainder of the property was equally divided between the two brothers. It was discovered that most of the properties were substantially mortgaged. My grandfather's brother, John Junior worked in Devonport Dockyard, had 5 children and did not enjoy good health. He was not a business man like his brother and was less than enthusiastic to take on mortgaged property in Cornwall. Some financial agreement was reached between the two brothers and my grandfather assumed responsibility for paying off the mortgages and arranging financial compensation to his brother, thus taking possession of all the property. This committed him to years of hard work.

I would describe my grandfather as a typically successful business man with one exception. He was modest, retiring, softly spoken and in direct contrast to his father, John Parkyn, who I have heard described as flamboyant, 'hail fellow', well met'. A man of strong character and personality.

My grandfather's reserved personality did however conceal a determined, adventurous, resourceful character, highly moral and compassionate, a staunch methodist, teetotaller, a Liberal of the Isaac Foot mould, respected and held rather in awe by his tenants, and the dock and clayworkers with whom he was constantly in contact at Par Harbour and at his shop. He was a worker for, and strong supporter of various charities, very active organising assistance and support for the Nursing Association. He was a member of a board responsible for education and schools in the district. He was a founder member of, and on the committee of the Par and district Brotherhood, a determined Christian organisation (more details appear in Grandfather Parkyn's Eclipse). He was a Trustee of Par Wesleyan Chapel (later renamed St Marys Methodist Church) a very active fund raiser for the chapel.

Grandfather was the main organiser of the PAR BEACH effort, an annual event we all looked forward to. A marquee was erected for the enjoyment of saffron bun and cream teas in the afternoon, a concert in the evening, followed by a pasty supper. There were sideshows and competitions and St Blazey Silver Band were in attendance. Some distinguished person, usually from the Methodist organisation, opened this popular event. Grandfather was the inspiration behind this and when he became too old to continue, the event did not survive for very long.

He was a freemason and a past member of St Andrews Lodge at Tywardreath. He was in some way associated with choral and orchestral circles, although he was not a singer or a musician. My mother (his daughter) was a violinist in the local orchestra so that was possibly the connection. It was through the Orchestral/Choral Society that Grandfather met and became friends with Mr and Mrs Felix George (no relation) and eventually with them set out on the remarkable journey from Par to Edinburgh in a Fiat tourer in 1927.

On this journey they viewed the 1927 Eclipse in Richmond Yorkshire. This was an example of his spirit of adventure. There are many examples and one in particular example was as a result of being left with large mortgage commitments. He had many competitors for the excellent business to be obtained from the ships that visited Par Harbour, unloading and loading cargo. He obtained some sort of official capacity whereby he had to sign bills of laden for the ships on the behalf of shipping agents, Couch and Co of Fowey. This brought him in direct contact with the ships captains and a good introduction to providing food and stores, ship's chandlery, oils, paints, ropes, lamps etc.

I still have the ancient binoculars he used from the balcony of his house with a panoramic sea view. He scanned the horizon at the crack of dawn for the first glimpse of a ship bound for Par, and then rushed, on foot, a mile or so to the docks to be there ahead of his competitors. I have been with him on several occasions waiting for a ship to enter the harbour. As soon as it was alongside, before it was moored or the gangplank fixed, I have seen him jump from the dockside on to the ships deck-no mean feat for a man in his sixties. He would get to see the Captain and steward first and often left the ship with an order before his rivals arrived.

He had a store on the dock for ship chandlery supplies but the shop for provisions was about a mile away. Stores were delivered from the shop to the ship on a large handcart with large iron bound wheels, packed with boxes of stores for at least 4-6 ships. The cart was so heavy it took two men to push it.

The shop was situated at crossroads. Opposite my grandfather's shop was another provision store in competition and yet another about 300 yards further down the road. During heavy rain the crossroads were prone to flooding as the area was low lying and had an inadequate draining system. I well remember during a prolonged flooding, the shops, now sandbagged, were inaccessible on foot. My grandfather brought a small boat on his handcart from the harbour and transported customers to and from his shop thus outwitting his competitors yet again! I well remember seeing him in thigh length waders pushing the boat Venice like from house to shop and back. I have seen small queues form at the water's edge for the novelty of shopping by boat!

I have fond memories of my grandfather and he greatly contributed to my happy childhood. We went regularly to chapel every Sunday morning. I would stand on the seat beside him so that we could share a hymn book. It was not a bore or a chore as he made as he made it all very interesting. I often walked with him hand in hand to the harbour. The memories of wonderment as a young child boarding the sailing ships and early steamers, meeting the Captains and crew, will always remain with me.

Grandfather Parkyn encouraged me in everything I did or aspired to do, giving me advice and practical assistance whenever possible. When I joined the RAF in 1942 he wrote to me regularly, always with encouragement. After the war I expressed my interest in showbusiness. He was far from enthusiastic, he would of preferred me to follow a more stable profession. The theatrical profession was frowned upon by Methodists. In spite if this he gave me £30 towards getting started - a considerable sum in 1947.

OTHER NOTES

He married and had two daughters Elizabeth and Sylvie (my mother). His first wife, Emma Hart, died of tuberculosis at about 30 years of age. Elizabeth was then about seven years and my mother only 18 months old.

His second wife was Jane Penrose Quick, daughter of either the Chief Coastguard or Harbour Master at Padstow. A sweet lady whom I knew as Grandma. She was the wife who accompanied him on his trip to Edinburgh and was a constant support to him all his life.

Grandfather Parkyn was in some way involved in recruiting and pensions during or after the first World War. During his lifetime he paid off all the mortgages and increased the properties by building 6 more houses. He was an avid reader of the Classics, Biographies and History and largely self-educated.

He spent a contented retirement, was a keen gardener and retained his interest in local affairs until his death in 1957 at the age of 87 years.

A DESCRIPTION by Mr. A.C. Parkyn of a tour by Motor Car from PAR to EDINBURGH and return, in 1927.

"Holiday". This word appeals to the worker – it may be from the physical aspect, or from mental fatigue, that those who labour with hand or brain desire what has become to many, an Annual Institution.

The constant strain on the worker in whatever realm of occupation needs change, rest, recreation. In travel the newness of each objective has its bearing on the mind; may-be of new thought, or hope, with its power of forgetting the claims of close attention which the earnest souls necessarily follows in their regular employment.

To us the prospect of a Motor Car touring holiday was the subject of many conversations, and thoughtful arrangements.

Our good friends Mr. & Mrs. George necessarily must have given much time, and have set their ingenious minds in the grove of imagination in deciding the routes to be followed, the places and towns of interest to be visited, and arrangements for rest and accommodation, for we learned that our objective was the line of totality of the Eclipse, and thence to Edinburgh. It was thus thought that our tour should have the dual pursuit of recreative and educational value; the reading of fragments of history, of places and plots laid so vividly in our best fiction, the opportunity it would give of visiting Cathedrals, Castles, Mansions, Cities and Towns; the thrill of travelling the busy roads of our beloved Country, viewing its fields and hedge-rows and natural scenic beauties, which Providence has so lavishly and prominently given to the Counties of Great Britain, each County being able to boast of the massiveness of its gifts, of valleys, hills and mountains, of its pastures and its ruggedness and of its pleasant people also. And in this respect, and after our return, we can gladly say we were not once disappointed. We Cornish people who have travelled through the pleasant land of Great Britain here report, that with every enquiry or conversation we derived pleasure, and was shown esteem. We can recall instances of kindliness which still contain pleasure, and memory recalls the dialects of each County, the mode of expression, the earnestness shown by gesture of hand or movement of body, the musical method of expression, especially so in Scotland with the Gaelic tongue.

Qualities were met with in our Journey, and at every halt in our adventure, that conveyed the Hall Mark of kindness and courtesy.

It will be necessary to leave at this point these landscapes and thoughts of the mind, and concentrate on the preparation for our tour and the needs of the journey.

As arranged, at 11 a.m. on Saturday the 25th June 1927 Mr. George and his "Fiat" were announced.

After warm salutation our tourist bags were strapped to the grid, and with the au-revoirs of our loved ones we made for our final start from Tywardreath.

We were soon ready, and lest we forget, we would mention that our touring party consisted of Mr. & Mrs. George, and Mr. & Mrs. Parkyn.

We left with the best hopes of our friends, and adieus of Miss Harris and Mary with their best wishes that we should have all the pleasure possible on our trip.

The Car started towards the historic Church, through the Village and up the Trenython Hill.

We did not give voluble expression to our thoughts at first, may-be they were directed to the Unseen with the prayer that His blessing and Presence would accompany throughout the coming days.

We also thought and appreciated the detailed interest for the individual comfort Mr & Mrs George had planned, and we in return had every confidence in our driver and his "Fiat".

Our first conversation was a suggestion that if casual notes and exchange of thoughts were expressed, it would serve to remind us of many incidents, things or places, on our journey, after our return.

We presume this is the one reason why these casual thoughts of memory are here submitted, and will help us to a better realisation of the eleven days of unique friendship, of mutual kindness, and all the qualities that make for good understanding.

Our Car was travelling very sweetly, and soon we reached Lostwithiel.

On nearing Boconnoc we had practically our only mishap to the tyres. Passing over a rough piece of road a tyre became punctured, but ten minutes sufficed in taking off the wheel and replacing with the spare.

With the expressed hope that we should not have a reoccurrence of this trouble we continued our journey, reaching Liskeard at 12-10. We stopped here for the repair of the puncture, and with the confidence that all the tyres were in good order and condition we proceeded toward Callington.

We could not pass here without enquiring for friends who hold a large place in Mr. & Mrs George's affection, and much esteemed by us. Memory's flash reminded us of the many pleasant years of social and other mutual work we had engaged in. We were all glad to learn that Mrs. Eustace was improving in health, and we left with the hope that her vigour would soon be restored. Friendships true and constant are great blessings; they give pleasure and reality to life.

We left Callington at 1:15 p.m. Passing through Gunnislake with the dis-used mined both on the hill and in the valley, with their huge burrows of refuse from the mine shafts and workings so noticeably reminding us of the activities of the past. These districts have done their best in providing ores and minerals for the requirement of the World's merchandise. Thus we thought of "Dear Old Cornwall" – "The Cornish Riviera" or as we prefer "Our Cornwall", as the land of minerals and radium, who has given her compliment of mining experts, and her brave men and boys in following the perilous mining industry in home and foreign Countries, proud of their calling, trained from youth to search and burrow for the hidden wealth that has to be mined from the bowels of the Earth, and in many Climes, thus adding their strength and ability in building up international prosperity and providing for the World's requirements in metals.

The Kit Hill was passed that stands so prominently near the boundary lime of the two Counties. Its towering height gives the impression of its being on guardian duty.

It is seen far down in the West, and from the Railway Carriages it presents a wild and rugged appearance. The view from this elevated road was beyond expression. If we were in search of beauty and scenery, we were well rewarded here. The River Tamar was showing its winding and Zig Zag course, the rocks of Morwelham, the shrubs and trees rising from the river banks up the steep cliffs to the hill-top. It presented a wondrous view with the craggy tops of the Devonshire Tors visible as we looked toward the sky-line, and at the bend of the River the Warships at their anchorage.

This panamonic view should gladden the heart, as nature and creation is displayed in all its wondrous forms.

We soon passed the boundary line of the Delectable Duchy, and realised by the sign-post that we were now on the roads of Glorious Devon.

Our next stop was by the road-side. Mr. George selected a pleasant and safe sport, with a high hedge on our left, sheltering us from the wind. The hedge provided us with luxurious growth of wild flowers, and ferns of many shades and varied tints of green. We all thought that an ideal spot had been chosen in which to open the Lunch baskets, which proved to be well laden. It was remarked that our friends had provided sufficient for the return journey.

After satisfying our need the brake was released, and our "Fiat" gave us to understand that she was anxious to continue with her load, comprising so much of Saint and sinner.

We passed through Tavistock at 2:25. We remembered the falls of her beautiful River, her Abbey ruins, Kelly's cottage, and her famous Market.

We soon reached Mary Tavy, and the Moors through Downtown and Surton. The elevation of the Moors was passed over was from 800 to 1050 feet. As our car rushed along the breeze was keen the air chilled our faces, but filled our lungs with its elixer, distilled by the long stretch of Moor. The clear defile of the many tors arrested the eye. We were amazed at the tremendous space of moorland, studded with bright yellow gorse, and the purple heather breaking into bloom.

We all enjoyed the thrill of racing over these Moors at a speed of 40 miles an hour, the expansive view, and the current of atmosphere with its purity and healing properties.

Okehampton was reached at 3 p.m. The main street was thronged with marketing people. Our impression was that our County towns not only provide for buying and selling, but gave an opportunity to the Farmer and lonely worker for social intercourse, and also of gaining the necessary information for competitive merchandise. We thought it was a pretty inland town, nestling under the heights of the rising Tors. The bracing district gave us an idea of its being good as a health resort.

We reached Exeter at 4 p.m. Its main streets were lined with people. We caught a glimpse of its 12th Century Cathedral.

We passed through Cullompton at 4:35, Wellington 5:10, Taunton 5:25 and reached Street at 6:20. We here enjoyed a cup of tea at the Bear Temperance Hotel. We next visited the Freinds' Meeting House, and were interested in its Library of well selected books.

The seats of the Meeting House were spotlessly clean, without paint or varnish. At the West end it had a raised platform and desk in the centre for Elders, and a space was provided at the entrance for free literature. The building itself was built with Quaker plainness, and for durability. It was very evident that those who planned its erection did not lose their ideal that they were erecting a House for the worship of God. Within the walled entrance was a large and beautiful Fir tree, showing its new growth of silver beauty. Not a weed was noticed in its clean kept sanded paths. At the back of the Meeting House was its burial ground, with its low semi-circular stones, all alike, marking the spot of the beloved who had entered into rest.

This place was sacred to our friends. We bowed our heads as Mrs. and Mr. George placed flowers, which they had brought from home, on their dearly beloved sister's grave with the intense feelings which can be imagined. We regarded it as an honour to be present in supporting our friends in their homage, their love and devotion, to the memory of their deceased sister.

We return to the Car, and in passing out of the town noticed the plain well dressed residents.

The Messrs Clarke, and other Companies, have here well built and commodious Boot and Shoe Factories. We were informed that the Owners of these works were of the Quaker persuasion, and we thought of Cadbury, Fry, Rowntree of Cocoa fame, who also had built large industries, had founded garden towns, had set world-wide examples as generous employers, and provided pleasant homes and conditions for their employees.

We may well think of them as solving the difficult problems as between employer and employee.

We reached Bristol at 9 p.m. Our friends were anxious to greet us, and provided us with home and rest on our first night.

We started from Bristol at 10:40 the following morning. It was then raining lightly, Our friends gave us all the best of wishes for an excellent time.

As our car rushed along the smooth even road we indulged in pleasant memories and inter-change of thoughts.

The long journey on the previous day of about 170 miles had not wearied us with tired feelings; the composing rest at the homely home of our Nephew and Niece, with all their thoughtful attention for our comfort, was considered as an added pleasure to our trip.

We passed the boundary line of the Counties of Gloucester and Wilts at Acton Tourville; a little later passing cross roads we made enquiries at a lonely cottage. We soon observed that we were addressing a gentleman with a strong Cockney accent. In reply to our questions he said he thought he was let down there by an aeroplane. It was one of the War problems. His getting back to his own border would be a welcome change. Farm work in a lone part was not desirable.

We soon sighted Swindon works in the hazy distance. We thought of many friends and experiences bound up with near and kindly relationships.

We soon passed another boundary stone at Coleshill, and were informed in the Berkshire dialect, by some lads who were resting by the road-side, that we were now travelling in their County.

Farrington was reached at 1:25, and Oxford at 2 p.m. As our Fiat entered the busy streets of Oxford we lifted our hats, and our ladies gracefully acknowledged the City and home of learning, famous in history as a University City "founded in the reign of Henry III on the site of certain Schools which were said to have been built by King Alfred". (This paragraph was taken from the Guide book.)

After finding our Hotel, garaging the Car, doing justice to a substantial lunch, we set out to see and seek information.

We accepted the offer of a guide, and were conducted to the sites of the following Colleges, viz., Merton, Baliol, Oriel, Queens, Corpus Christi, All Souls and others.

We also visited the Bodlian Library, and other buildings of interest and fame.

We did not forget it was Sunday, and having regard for our great privileges and duties we all attended service at Christ Church, the Cathedral of Oxford. We enjoyed the singing, and the resounding tones of the massive organ. We noticed the reverend attitude of the worshippers in prayer and service.

We had hoped to have listened to a sermon from a Professor, Dignatory or Bishop, but were disappointed in this, the service being practically all choral, without an address.

We had the pleasure later in the evening of listening to the well trained Choir, who sang for an hour. It was a chilly evening.

Chairs were provided for the audience on the broad parapet, where they sat and listened to the end. This to us was a very pleasant hour.

The Choir sang from the steps leading to the Audience Room of the College. The tone of the boys' voices was strong, musically clear and as one voice. The balance of the other parts was equally good. All the unaccompanied part songs that were rendered were taken from ancient classical music.

These boys, we were informed, were selected from the home of Oxford.

A pause was made in the service at 9 p.m. in obeisance to "Great Tom", the bell said to be the thirty first largest in the World, and weighing 17,640 lbs. Its clapper weighs 342 lbs.

Every night at 9:5 the bell tolls a Curfew of 101, the signal for closing the various College Gates. On this Sunday night it gave a peal of 21 only, in honour, I presume, of the musical evening held within its College Gates.

Our thought was as we left the University square, could not this be done in our own district, with its musical ability. Naturally, one's thoughts revert to one's own district, with the desire for actual progress in the realms of attainments, or ideals.

We later noticed these boys accompanying their Conductor presumably to his home; by their manner they evidently held him in affectionate esteem.

When visiting the University Halls in the afternoon, inspecting the wonderful architecture and design of these noble buildings, we admired the ceilings, wonderful in design and execution; windows with their Binlical illustrations in the original glass from the 12th and 13 Centuries, with their radiant colours and blendings; the carved seats and furniture showing the colour of age and use, and many otherbeautiful objects representing the art of carving etc. in the 11th, 12t, and 13th. Centuries.

We must not forget to mention a picture hung in one of the large Halls, which claimed our attention. The subject was "Touch me not for I have not yet ascended. It was the work of a celebrated master of the

13th Century. The face and figure of Christ, the pathos that met our gaze, portraying the Majesty and Love of the Redeemer.

We thought Artists in revealing their mind in their paintings must be guided by inspiration, or the vision of the Soul.

In passing the lofty corridors to the Dining Hall the walls on all sides were hung with paintings of Fellows or Celebrities who had passed through the College, and had attained national fame and position in the various spheres of the Realm as representing Church, State, Law, Science, Art, Literature, and various other commanding service of their Country.

One could not fail to discern the hall mark of high purpose characterised in each protrait. What an influence these paintings of men who had gained University distinction, and then National honour by their life's achievements, exercise on the past and present students who are privileged to study or use this Hall under the gaze of these paintings.

The few hours in thes beautiful City were, we hoped, well engaged, and our mental outlook was concentrated in the beauty and attractions that our afternoon and evening gave us.

Thus our second day ended with these thoughts.

At breakfast the following morning the scenes of yesterday were pleasantly chatted over. The ladies suggested that at some future date it would be well to spend at least a week here. They were certain we should all anjoy it. Anticipation for pleasantness spells enjoyment. May-be we all made secret promises for some time or days in the future, but we were cautious not to make definite promises. Experience has taught us that we may have other and more important claims for future consideration.

We started from our Hotel at 10:15 a.m., passed the Tower of Oxford Castle, Baliol College, and stopped at the Martyrs' Memorial. It occupies a central position, and stands for Faith and Courage, showing that martyrdom cannot alter the deeper life.

Latimer's last words were "Be of good comfort, Master, Ridley, and play the man. We shall this day light such a candle, by God's Grace, in England, as I trust shall never be put out".

The following inscription is engraved on the Memorial:–
"To the Glory of God and in grateful commemoration of His Servants, Thomas Cranmere, Nicholad Ridley, Hugh Latimer, Prelates of the Church of England, who near this spot yielded their bodies to be burned, bearing witness to the sacred truths which they had affirmed, and against the errors of Rome, and rejoicing that to them was given not only to believe in Christ, but also to suffer for His sake. This monument was erected by public subscriptions MDCCCXLI."

YELVERTON

A PORTION OF THE SOUTH FRONT

OXFORD, BALLIOL COLLEGE & MARTYRS MEMORIAL

OXFORD, VIRGIN PORCH,
ST. MARY'S CHURCH

OXFORD, CHRIST CHURCH

OXFORD,
MARTYS' MEMORIAL

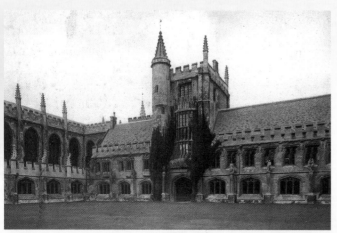

OXFORD, MAGDALEN COLLEGE, FOUNDERS TOWER & CLOISTER

Bishops Latimer and Ridley suffered Martrydom October 16th. 1553, and Archbishop Cranmere March 21st. 1556.

As we again continued our journey we were not concerned in not receiving acknowledgement of ability or qualification from the Universities, but the City gave us Degrees of Pleasant Memory.

If time had permitted we should have enjoyed a visit to the River, Parks and many other places of renowned interest.

In motoring out of the City we passed some very beautiful Houses and Estates; the landscapes also presented a wooded appearance.

At 11:30 we stopped at the busy market town of Banbury, made famous by the nursery rhyme of "Ride a White Horse to Banbury Cross" etc. This Cross stands in the centre of the town; no doubt it is more interesting to visitors than residents.

The Church tower of rather peculiar design was visible about half a mile to the left of our road.

Post Cards, and home-made Banbury cakes were purchased; the former were despatched to our anxious home friends, and Cake were enjoyed by the roadside.

As we motored out of the town we passed many old and picturesque Houses, and on the border we had the peculiar co-incidence of meeting a white horse being taken to the town, may-be to the cross.

As our "Fiat" sped on its way we at a distance noticed a tall wireless standard, and presumed it was Daventry. Who does not know of Daventry? We cannot think of a single newspaper which has not its Daventry Wireless News Column.

We reached here at 12:5, and followed the main road to the wireless station. It is situated on the hill, and about 1/4 of a mile from the main road. Our photographer ventured into a field so as to get an un-interrupted view for his focus; these snaps of scenes and places will help us to convey objects that gave us charm and satisfaction, and will give us refreshed memories on our return. They will also help us to re-produce pleasure to our enquiring friends.

The station we at first thought was disappointing. It did not possess the massiveness that we had expected. We agreed that the wireless experts in the building knew what was required, and arranged accordingly. It was constructed with two standards, one much higher than the other, with wire connections. The re-laying office, or works, was situated between the two poles. We were informed later that the highest pole measureed 500 feet from the surface.

Our conversation as we returned to the quiet town ran somewhat in this groove :– Daventry's wireless programme appears in practically all daily papers; imagine the interest of the enthusiasts of all ages who search for this column; we think of wireless as one of the best or greatest popular educators that has ever been perfected, it brings the same lessons, may-be from the Preacher, Lecturer, Vocal or Instrumentalist, both to the Mansion and Cottage, who can measure its influence etc.

We then purchased writing and posted view cards to our friends, assuring them that we were safe from the current of Ether.

We knew that sounds, voices and music were floating around us. Our natural hearing was not yet attuned; may-be a new generation may arise that will possess this faculty, and will not need the necessary apparatus as now employed.

We now moved forward for Rugby, and entered the town at 1:15. We were all well tuned for Lunch, and were well catered for at an Hotel.

We enjoyed listening to the general conversations at our resting places. Here we were in the company of Farmers, Merchants, and Professional men. The subjects here were various; crops and prospect of harvest, business problems, the expectancy of weather conditions for the Eclipse etc.

Our thoughts also were of the Eclipse, and our hope of seeing the Corona.

Being at Rugby we were all anxious to see at close vision the towering spars that we saw at a distance. This immense wiereless Station was about a mile from the town. We were well repaid for our visit. The immense height of the iron standards; 850 feet, I think, the amount and size of the tackling and stays. We counted 12 of the gigantic columns in two perfectly straight lines. The network of wires and accessories that we presumed was necessary or needed for the perfecting of the system. Here, too, the buildings were in the centre. No doubt they contained huge machinery for working the electric plant.

We had great satisfaction in viewing so closely this wonderful erection laid with methematical accuracy. It is apparently on a larger scale than the wireless Beam erection on our Goss Moor. We left here at 2:35.

As we sped forward our thoughts and conversation reverted to the wireless, and the rapid strides it has made, assisted at Sientests sich as Lodge and many others, who have added the result of their laboratory re-search; the present development of the Beam system by

9

Marconi. Who can say that these men were not created for this great purpose, which may yet be the instrument or means of instituting a common universal language, as we link up our Colonies and the uttermost parts of the World.

It is the means of proclaiming internatinal Brotherhood, and Peace and Good-will.

We are glad our County has taken its part; Poldhu was selected and used as the first high power station for the Atlantic service.

Our next call was Lutterworth. We visited John Wycliffe Church, and inspected the tablet placed to his memory. It was here, as Rector of the Church, that he finished his translation of the Bible.

It is well known that he held to the principles of the Reformation, and on that account was regarded with enmity by the Roman Catholic leaders. The date of his death was 1384.

We next proceeded to Leicester, arriving there at 4:5 p.m. The car was garaged here for an hour.

We made our way to a first class Restaurant. It was evident that Tea was regarded as a friend; indeed the young waitress served us in good style, and with pleasant smiles. We were refreshed, and enjoyed our walk in the busy streets.

Mr. George remained with the car, and gave it necessary attention. We did not forget the gentleman we were so dependent on, and it was our pleasure to bring him Leicester fruit and cakes; his appreciation was accepted as a pleasant reward.

The hour spent here was much enjoyed. We noticed the smart window dressing. In the business house and street there appeared to be the quick kindly tone. We later had proof of this. We classed it as one of the smartest towns we had passed through.

When starting from the Garage our instructions were to follow certain streets. Following these we came to a very busy thorough-fare. The policeman on point duty gave us the signal to stop. We approached him requesting reason for this, when he stated very definitely that we were in a one-way street, and must return. In response we said we were directed that way, and were strangers. He promptly enquired where we had come from. We answered "Cornwall", when he said "Alright, come along"; the traffic of the street which was very heavy, was accordingly stopped until our Fiat passed.

What induced this policeman to give us such consideration. Was it not the magic word "Cornwall"? We venture to say 'Yes'.

Our thoughts reflected pleasure in passing out of the beautiful City of Leicester. The home, and famous for its Hosiery, and kindly people.

Cardinal Wolsey was buried here at the Leicester Abbey.

History informs us that he lost the favour of Henry VIII, from being a great personage was humbled, and died a broken dejected man. Among his last words were "If I had served God "as dilligently as I have done my King, He would not have given me over in my grey hairs."

As our motor passed out of the City towards Loughborough we noticed on our right a large Rose Nursery. Gardeners were intent on their work, presumably dis-budding in order to give the purchaser better and stronger bushes for the coming season's planting, or they were may-be budding young stock with the latest novelties of the "Queen of the Garden".

Every profession or trade has a science attached to its progress; long periods of thought and experiment are given by the scientific gardener in hybridous work, and producing or improving floral novelties.

We regard gardening as one of the Royal and most ancient occupations.

We passed through Loughborough at 5:15. This is a Hosiery manufacturing town. We had very kind thoughts as we remembered the Revd. D.R. Robson, M.A. late Vicar of Par, who is now Vicar of one of the large Churches here.

At 6:5 we were passing through the crowded streets of Nottingham. This was one of the largest, and apparently business towns we had visited.

We must not forget that John Player & Sons have their Tobacco and Cigarettes Factory here. It is also the centre of the Lace industry.

It was very interesting to notice the large crowds travelling on the pavement, and who congregate in the Public Squares or spaces, or moving to-wards the Parks.

The streets were laid with stone cobble, and appeared equally thronged with motor vehicles as the pavements with pedestrians.

The Policeman at all branch streets, and busy thoroughfares, and in every town, evoked our sympathy by their patience and constant thought in directing the traffic, and thus preventing disastrous collisions. They use of eye, hand, and arm with the white gauntlet was seemingly obeyed and respected by all motorists. We can easily label these officers as the hardest worked men we met on our tour.

Part of the country from Nottingham to Gainsborough was very beautiful. Passing Ollerton the road led us through the Dukeries. Plantations of Firs and other ornamental and stately trees formed almost an avenue for apparently several miles.

We enjoyed the sweetly laden odorous atmosphere. As the Car carried us through this rich scene of sylvean beauty each of us drank deeply from it sweetness.

In questioning ourselves, why this verdant growth and perfume from these trees that rejoice and wave their branches with every breeze; we think of the juices these trees obtain from the soil, their absorbing into sectional powers for growth and further establishing its roots. Its power of distilling its odour from the liquid of sap, leaf and flower, and so quietly discharging its purifying and sweetening perfumes, for the pleasures and healing of man, beast and bird. It is not to Switzerland that many take the weakness of body, that they may partake of the healing qualities of the Noble Fir. Often we hear of Bournemouth's avenues of Firs and their healing virtue.

Many thoughts came to us as we passed through this famous part.

The homes and residences of Noble Lords and Ladies were here.

We noticed several groups, who had travelled by car, enjoying the Picnic under the spreading trees.

We reached Gainsborough at 8:20 p.m. On the way we noticed several scattered Coal Mines, with their high framework, and Pit winding apparatus.

When entering the town by crossing a wide bridge over the River Trent, we were informed by the Gate Keeper that a toll of 3/- was the fee for crossing the Bridge.

We had thought we were on the King's highway, but evidently Gainsborough rejoices in her private as well as public rights and claims.

Our fee was paid, and we enquired of him our nearest route to Epworth. He, with quiet Yorskhire style and dialect, informed us that we must turn back to yon crossing and take the main road. We were obliged for his direction, but he did not return the toll.

We thought probably there is a contrast between a Yorkshire and Cornish man; we need not follow the moral, neither the evidence or verdict.

We were now on the Lincolnshire roads again.

In several places on the route the roads were above the level of the field, and would suggest swamp in winter.

It is June month, the length of day suitable for evening travel.

The country here was well cultivated, and crops looked healthy. It suggested by the appearance of the fields that the Lincolnshire Farmer knew his job, and was not afraid of work. The fields of Beans and Peas were new to us as a farm crop.

On nearing Epsworth our attention was attracted to fields with quite a number of different crops, which ran in spaces from end to end.

We arrived at Epsworth at 9 p.m.

We found our home for rest, which had been kindly arranged for us by the resident Wesleyan Minister, garaged the Car, and had a good wash and brush up.

By this time our hostess had prepared a real Lincolnshire tea. We all enjoyed the home-prepared food, and soon forgot the long distance we had travelled, but not the road-side and other beauties.

Our host and hostess gave us of their best, not only in comfort, but conversation and history. He was from over the border of the Trent; no doubt attracted many years ago by our motherly hostess with her kind manner, and to us, musical tone of speech, and even now fair to look upon as an aged mother. We can imagine the far off days when to our hostess he was the beau ideal, and to him she possessed the beautiful and queenly look and ways which appealed and won their hearts, and decided their future; hence he crossed the River and made Epsworth the venue of his life-work, pulling or rowing together and now the General Dealers Shop on one side of their premises and the accommodation for Refreshements on the other side, with this motherly lady attending to our keen needs.

Our host, an intelligent man, gave us interesting information of the ways and manners of the district. He spoke strongly in favour of the Lincolnshire farmers as industrious, and equal to – if not the best – farmers in England, of their system of small holdings, and the success made of them, emphasizing that every yard of ground of soil had to make its return of crop and revenue; the fishing on the Trent; the trade by boat or lighter from Hull or Goole; the difference of carriage on heavy goods as between Railway and Lighter.

It was now time for rest, as we had decided to be on the trek early the following a.m., for we were now at Epsworth, the home of the Wesley's fame and influence, and with the request for an early breakfast, and good night to our friends we retired for needed rest.

We were all astir early the next morning, and had breakfast consisting of Lincolnshire bacon, eggs, butter, bread, toast and other substantial and sweet foods and dainties, and even connoisseurs of Tea would have declared "Good" had they been fortunate enough to have joined us at the breakfast table.

After satisfying the need that promotes vigour we tried to out-line our programme for the morning, and in doing this we had the assistance of our host, who informed us of Wesley's Memorial Church, and of their Choir gaining the Gold Medal at the singing festival at Leeds; that his daughter was the assistant organist at the Church.

Our first duty was to call on the Wesleyan Minister, the Revd. and present him with our gratitude for the kindly arrangements he had made for our comfort. We called at the Manse, and were informed by his kindly wife that in obedience to an urgent connectional call he had left early for Manchester. She conveyed his message of regret, and kind regards, with the hope – in which they mutually joined – that we should enjoy our visit.

Nothing would satisfy the good lady unless we would permit her to show us around the Church and buildings, including the Manse.

The Church is similarly designed to Newquay, Gothic structure with a tall steeple, stained glass windows, pitch-pine seats, and covered and made comfortable for reading; a circular pulput with a beautiful stained glass window in the West, also a gallery in the west end.

Facing the entrance door a tablet was erected to the memory and work of the Founder of Methodism.

A very valued Communion table was shown us, valued because of its association and historic interest.

This table was used at the Parish Church by Samuel Wesley. Apparently many years ago the Church altar was repaired and renovated, the Contractor supplying another communion table with permission to take this one as part of the contract. It was then used in the Contractor's office as a writing table.

After the Memorial Church was built, one of the leading Methodists of London heard of the report and immediately set agencies at work, the honoured table was discovered and purchased, and again dedicated to the Service of God in the Memorial Church. Its appearance shows it to be an aged Oak table in perfect condition.

We thought of the association, Is not its real value in the fact that from this table the Bread and Wine was taken, and the command "Do this in remembrance of me". Who can measure the inspiration of these services, and the influence on the lives of the sons of Samuel Wesley.

The schoolroom was adjoining the Church, and we should say from its furnished equipment, its Kitchen, cooking untensils and conveniences for Teas, quarterly meetings, or synods, Organ, Piano, everything necessary was provided.

The Manse formed a part of the enclosed square, with garden and shrubbery in line with the street.

We signed our names in the Church Visitors' Book.

The Caretaker, who was also a Class Leader, informed us that his eldest daughter was residing at St. Austell, having met her husband when he was billeted at Epsworth during the War.

A letter was written by the Minister's wife to the Vicar requesting him to give us facilities to visit the Rectory or Vicarage.

EPSWORTH CROSS

WINDMILL, EPSWORTH

SAMUEL WESLEYS' TOMB, EPSWORTH

ST. ANDREWS CHURCH, EPSWORTH

JOHN & CHARLES WESLEYS' MEMORIAL CHURCH

John Wesley and his great work has been recalled by speakers on the Union of Methodism. This picture by Wm. Hatherell, R.I., shows Wesley preaching from the steps of a Market Cross. Thousands gathered to hear the man who delared "The world is my parish" wherever thus apostle of the Gospel chose to speak in town, village and church. Augustine Birrell likened his energy as a travelling preacher to that of a man conducting a General Election without the help of any colleague. It was not unusual for thousands to wait patiently for the arrival on horseback of this great Evangelist. His journeyings and experiences are narrated in his famous Journal, which has never lacked readers. It has been computed that John Wesley preached on 40,000 occasions and travelled 5,000 miles a year—a record in those days.

REV SAMUEL WESLEYS' TOMBSTONE

JOHN WESLEYS' RESCUE WINDOW

REV SAMUEL WESLEYS' TOMBSTONE

RECTORY, EPSWORTH

We next visited the Town Cross. The steps were much worn with use and age.

John Wesley often preached from the steps of this Cross. Photographs were taken with Mr. & Mrs. Parkyn standing on each side of the pillar.

We then went to the Parish Church. We thought it badly needed renovation.

We stood by Samuel Wesley's grave.

Photograph of Mr. George was taken here.

Then to the Vicarage; to our disappointment the Vicar was engaged. He sent us word of regret and enquired if we could call later in the day, but our time was limited, and a lady of the house acted as guide. We were shown the window from which John Wesley was rescued from the fire. Photographs of the window, and of the Vicarage were taken.

We talked on the Lawn and garden. Our thoughts led us back when the Wesleys occupied the vicarage, and of the games played here, of the study of life's work.

The Vicarage is at a distance from the Church, and at the entrance to the town. From the Rescue wondow it gives a view of the Church, town and district. May it not be from this window that the thought was born which has become famous through Methodism – "The World is my Parish" – a great idealism formed in the mind has become, may we say, the romance of the Wesleyan Church.

Hugh Price Hughes, in his presidential address, said that it was not Wesley, but Christ himself, that founded the Methodist Church. He then claimed the honour for Wesley of being appointed by God as His instrument, and claiming for Wesley the honour of being divinely appointed for the World-wide evangilisation, and the means of preaching the Gospel of Christ to every Nation and people.

It is worthy of note that the late President of America, Dr. Wilson, in a Lecture on the life and work of John Wesley, said his life for Christ was of untiring enthusiasm, and of unremitting insistency. He said no stranger at an Inn, no traveller met upon the road left him without hearing of his business.

The Minister of to-day, if he is to reach the ear of men, must be what John Wesley was "deeply conversant with the "natures of his fellow men, and with a keen power of conviction. Granted that, the Minister can do for another age what John Wesley did for the 18th Century."

Before passing on we should like to re-produce the inscription on the Memorial Stone at the Memorial Church, viz :–

"Sacred to the Memory of Revd. John Wesley, M.A., some-time Fellow of Lincoln College, Oxford. Was born at Epsworth June 17th,

1903, son of the Revd. Samuel Wesley, M.A. and his wife Susannah, by whom he was prayerfully educated in the things of God. He died in London March 2nd, 1791, in the full triumph of faith after 65 years of un-remitting and successful ministerial toil, aged 89 years."

We were glad of this visit or pilgrimage to the home of one of England's greatest influences. His was an effective bearing on every class and condition of the Empire. There was always present that reforming note, and this mission he proclaimed, from his revered father's tombe stone, the Epsworth Cross, at public places in the streets and lanes, from early morn to late at night, with a strenousness that could only be derived from the eternal source of all life.

Who has not read of his journeys in Cornwall, of his oppositions, rebukes, chastisements, of the lack of resting places, and hunger, of the closed Church doors. He had his reward.

He preached the Kingdom of God, the saving Truth of Faith, and he won the hearts of rich and poor. His appeal to the masses throughout England is said to have worked the prevention of Revolution as was being fought in France at that period.

With the thrill of passing thoughts that we were in Epsworth, had walked its streets, had converse with its people, had stood on the Cross where Wesley had commenced his adventure "after his Soul had become strangely warmed", had visited the Lawn and garden, and viewed the Escape Window which still carries the marks of the Fire.

Epsworth, the town itself, we thought could not have been larger in population than St. Blazey, and very like Tywardreath in formation.

Our car was again ready for advance. We lingered as long as possible with our friends.

We may remark here that good-will and friendship was a principle we tried to follow in every home that gave us shelter, and with people that we met. In this we gained friends, confidences, and kindnesses which added greatly to our pleasures.

We started for Selby at 12:25, arriving there after a pleasant run at 1:30. After Lunch we explored a portion of the town. A rather massive Cross occupied a position in the square leading to the Abbey. We enquired from a Policeman the meaning of the Cross, and were informed that it was a 14th Century Butter Cross, and with native wit pointed to a rusty knife (which had probably been left there by children), suggesting that the knife had been left there by the builders at its erection. Our reply was that if that were so Selby had nutured many generations of honest folk.

The Abbey was well worth visiting; the immense edifice revealed age and decay in many places.

We again continued our journey, leaving at 3:20, and were speeding forward for the famous City of York.

Large posters announcing York Minster's 1300 Anniversary were posted in many prominent places, and met us as we passed through the busy streets.

We could not resist attending this service. Accordingly our car was garaged.

On entering the building we were impressed with the great length and height of the Minister, and the large audience of reverent worshippers, together with the wonderfully toned Organ and the quality of the augmented Choir.

The Bishop's voice sounded to the ends of the Minster, but it was so blurred by space that we failed to get the message, or follow the learned Prelate in his address.

This festival Anniversary was to continue the whole week.

We left York at 4 p.m. by one of its ancient gateways; we noticed its turreted walls.

Our conversation as we sped on to Northallerton was on the magnificence of the service at the Minster; the quality of the boy soprano voices that filled the building with a volume of music. The Choir itself was an organ. We shall inevitably forget many scenes and pleasures, but the music of the Choir, we hope, will often return to us with both the whispers and crashing notes of that noble organ. We were informed that a celebrated American organist was at the key-board on that day.

We arrived at Northallerton at 6:15, and with frankness said we were ready for tea.

We were soon served at the Hotel with the beverage that satisfies, the Cup of cheer that radiates pleasure and induces conversation.

We were well served with Eggs, Bread and Butter, and other dainties.

Our thoughts whilst at the tea-table were directed to the event of which we were hoping to witness from the line of totality the following morning.

Our thoughts too, were "What of the night"?

Our proposal was to sleep in the Car by the road-side, or on some vantage ground. We had to prepare requirements, such as sandwiches, thermos with hot tea and milk etc.

We decided to get all refreshments packed here.

During our chat at the tea-table, a gentleman who was sitting at a distance from us enquired if we were from Cornwall. He thought we were Cornish by our dialect. He had received a great deal of pleasure from the Cornish folk during the Great War, when he was stationed at a Fort near Plymouth for 3 years. His home was in Derbyshire.

It was an evident pleasure to each of us to meet a stranger who could lead us back in thought to our own County, and speak of pleasures, friendships and kindly experiences with the sound of gratitude in his voice.

We left for Darlington at 7:55 p.m.

We had learned ere this that experiences of a varied nature cross the travellers path.

When about 4 miles from Darlington we noticed a Car stopped by the road-side. On nearing the spot we saw two men standing on the grass, attending to a young man who appeared unconscious.

We alighted, and were soon at their side offering help. We did what we could in the form of first-aid, gave him a stimulant and warm tea.

After a time he told us in broken sentences that he was on his way to Newcastle; he had been cycling the whole day and became dizzy and fell from his cycle. We thought it a case in which the young fellow had used all vigour, and had dropped from his machine in sheer exhaustion.

After a conference with our friends it was decided that they would take him to Darlington, and request the Police to arrange for Hospital treatment.

We followed the good Samaritans, and promised to see them at the Police Offices.

We reached Darlington at 9 p.m., interviewed the Chief Officer of Police and gave our statement.

After a general conversation in which he informed us that he had just returned from a motoring tour in Cornwall, he advised us to go to Richmond for the Eclipse, saying many Darlington folk would be going there. Richmond was about 10 miles distant.

After further chat he gave us advice as to how we should act should we met with a similar case whilst on our trip.

Our interest was such that we promised to enquire the following morning.

We decided to accept the Officer's advice, and our Car sped towards our objective.

Fortune favours the brave ... passing a farm-gate we noticed a young man, and halted to enquire the distance to Richmond. He replied about one and a half miles, and then said they had many Cars and people at their Farm on the hill, who were staying the night, sleeping in the Cars or in tents, and that only a small charge was being made for the convenience. He also said he could arrange bed-room accommodation for the ladies.

We soon arrived at a decision, and our car mounted the steep hill leading to the Farm.

After inspection of the Yard we selected a place of shelter for the Car.

We considered that we had been well guided in having the offer of night accommodation, especially as we were now on the totality line.

We learned later that this was one of the best positions in the district in which to view the Eclipse.

We escorted the ladies to the Cottage, and had the pleasure of knowing they were comfortably cared for. This thought more than compensated us for any inconvenience we might have to encounter.

We returned to the Car, and placed our rugs in order.

It was now about 11 p.m. The light had faded, and the cattle had apparently composed themselves.

We could hear our companions of the open veldt in their chat and laughter.

It occurred to us that a brisk walk in the field in the bracing air would help for rest and possible sleep.

As we passed through the Yard into the field we were met by the same farm worker who had invited us to this spot earlier in the evening.

As we walked the field our conversation was on various topics. We soon discovered we were in the company of a studious young man. He gave us his experiences of the War, his return home, his difficulty in getting employment, and of his ultimately having to accept farm service.

He praised the Farmer and his household – one of the best of Farmers and kind-ness itself to his employees. He expected every man to do a full day's work for his day's pay, and other observations enlivened us on our mid-night walk.

It was now getting very chilly; we were probably 1000 feet above sea-level.

As we re-traced our steps we noticed the Military Camp at Catterick. It looked very pretty with its twinkling lights. Our friend said that often of an evening they tried to count the lights, but how-ever many were counting them they could not bring the same number.

Looking to-wards a point of the Great North Road the lights of passing cars were simply continuous, and apparently hurrying to Richmond.

After bidding our friend "Good-night", and expressing our hope for a cloudless morning we returned to our Car, arranged our comfortable rugs and tried to compose ourselves in order to enjoy nature's remedy for physical and nervous exhaustion, for we remembered we had had a long travel with many incidents on the road.

We also noticed that our camping friends, not a distance from us, had become quiet and we presumed they were in dream-land.

After about 2 hours rest in which we often reached the point of forgetfulness, we discovered that the perfect sill-ness of the night was not to prevail. A lady wearing heavy boots was making a constant round journey of the Yard, and in doing so did not exercise the least regard for the would-be sleepers. On entering the yard the heavy gate was opened full, and then allowed to slam with a creaking sound. This was repeated many times during the night, and we soon discovered our thoughts were not kindly towards this disturber of sleep.

We had about 4 hours of sleep in the Car, for which we were very thankful.

At day-break the stir throughout the Camp was general, and in a short time the field was the scene of an animated crowd.

All were anxious and conferring with each other on the great question that had brought or induced them to be present.

At 4:15 a number of young scientists trooped into the field, each carrying an instrument or stand of some description, and were soon taking up positions suitable for their instruments and observations.

We also discovered our lady night-walker, no doubt very exhausted, now sitting very cosily on her case, smoking a cigarette and evidently interested in the engagements of the field.

We noticed the young students fixing an aerial to one of the trees from their broad-casting apparatus and loud speaker, which was to adjusted that time and information could be received from Greenwich.

Telescopes on tripods, light refractors, star plans, and demonstrators were so arranged that at the time of the Eclipse all would be readiness. Each student was provided with College forms for making reports of their observations. We were informed that these young men had been selected by their College in Rutlandshire for this purpose.

As we moved to the centre of the field we were charmed with the mist rising slowly with apparent gentleness up the hillside. We do not remember ever seeing Nature's mantle in this beautiful form, its shading of dark grey at the bottom becoming lighter as it ascended, so even in texture and transparency, and as the red haze of the sun's rays was reflected on this mantle from the valley we were thankful for the view or scene of nature's way, so gorgeous and perfect, from the summit of the hill.

We were all looking towards the East, hoping that the clouds which were coming up on either side would disperse before the time of the Eclipse.

We noticed, too, that clouds, said to be 1500 feet high, appeared to be stationery.

As the moments of expectancy advanced anxiety became more intense, for the clouds were still rising and presented themselves as a bank of mist.

The loud speaker could be heard giving time and signals.

For a brief space of time was saw the early part of the Eclipse through a rent or hollow in the clouds, just the crescent.

As the sun became obscured by the passing of the dark body of the moon the atmosphere became cold, the light was dimmed, the colour of the grass and objects became strange, with a violet colour hue; the cattle and farm stock a few minutes earlier carried on their usual bleat, but now became very quiet.

We watched the dark angry looking cloud come up from the South East.

We noticed the purple shade on each person as a coloured gown, and the stillness that prevailed during these 23 seconds. Even the Loud Speaker as it sounded the time and progress of the Eclipse seemed as an intruder; the time appeared as minutes instead of seconds.

As the Sun in her course passed the interruption the light returned, the chilliness passed, the greyness was absorbed by the

NEWMINSTER ABBEY, MORPETH

EDINBURGH CASTLE, VIEW FROM ARGYLE TOWER

EDINBURGH CASTLE, THE BANQUETING HALL

THE FORTH BRIDGE, SCOTLAND

HOLYROOD PALACE AND ARTHUR SEAT, EDINBURGH

EDINBURGH CASTLE AND ESPLANADE

THE HEATHER ISLAND

STEAMER ON LOCH LOMOND

*EDINBURGH CASTLE, REGENT
MORTONS GATEWAY, EAST SIDE*

LOCH LOMOND

re-kindled light, the green of the grass and trees was restored, and the birds and beats resumed their natural life.

It was soon evident that this eventful phenomena had passed.

Each went quietly to their tent or car, the students with their scientific instruments were busy in safely packing for their return journey, and ourselves with our thoughts and impressions summoned courage for enquiry.

We were anxious to know what the effect was on our College friends, as earlier in the morning we had conversation with each of them.

In reply to our enquiry "Are you disappointed with the "result of the Eclipse and your observations", the "No" was very distinct. They had hoped for a clear view of th Eclipse, they would have liked to have seen the stars that the phenomena would make it possible to scan, they would have liked to have taken the density of light in the natural conditions of the Eclipse, and their telescopes could not trace the heavens because of the clouds.

The wireless expert student was referred to in all enquiries as "Marconi".

The thanks of the crowd was won by his ingenious command of the apparatus, the full tone was given to the loud-speaker by his manipulation, which kept the whole camp informed with the time, progress and general information of the Eclipse.

Our Mr. George had the honour of presenting our compliments and thanks to "Signor Marconi" on the success and the natural adaptation of his instrument for the benefit and information of all, saying whatever else failed it was not the Marconi instrument. His was one pleasing effect of the morning; his acknowledgment was pleasing because of his reserve and hesitancy.

Each student, when questioned, assured us that to them it was a great time, valuable data had been gained, the mind had been enlarged, and the eye had had a wonderful vision.

These young men entered the field with merriment and laugther; they departed with a thoughtful and serious mind, and we think this was the effect on the whole company. Each appeared to be communing with their own thoughts, conversation was not resumed quickly. Questions were replied to in quiet tones.

No doubt the 19th Psalm was remembered "The heavens declare the Glory of God; and the firmament sheweth his handiwork. Day unto day uttereth speech, and night unto night sheweth knowledge."

We returned to the Shepherd's cottage. The restless night, our early rising and excitement, the keen air of the morning, also the active thoughts which had its bearing on the mind, made the breakfast table possess a singular attraction to us.

We all needed the cup of hot tea and stimulating food.

But we wanted most to hear each other's voice, to learn each other's experience. It was simply a time of placing our thoughts on the breakfast table, for we remembered we had travelled from distant Cornwall for this occasion.

It was evident that a permanent impression had been made on each, which could not be easily effaced from memory.

We thought all observers were disappointed in not having a view of the Corona.

We had previously read Sir Robert Ball's "Story of the Heavens" (page 62) which shows photographic views of this wonderful solar phenomena, and at various places and periods. Who has not read his wonderful description of the Sun's power and liberality of heat and light. We think a digression here will help us by quoting from page 68 :—

"The Earth can only graps the merest fraction of light and heat, less than the 2,000,000,000 part of the whole".

"The Sun's gracious beams supply the magic power than enables the Corn to grow and ripen. It is the heat of the Sun which raises water from the ocean in the form of vapour, and then sends down that vapour as rain to refresh the earth, and to fill the rivers which bear our ships down to the sea.

"It is the heat of the sun beating on the large continents which gives rise to the breezes and winds that waft our vessels across the deep; and when on a winter's evening we draw round the fire and feel its invigorating rays, we are only enjoying sunbeams which shone on the earth countless ages ago.

"The heat in those ancient sunbeams developed the mightly vegetation of the coal period, and in the form of coal that heat was slumbered for millions of years, till we now call it again into activity. It is the power of the sun stored up in coal that urges on our Steam engines. It is the light of the sun stored up in coal that beams from every gas light in our cities. For the power to live and move for the plenty with which we are surrounded, for the beauty with which nature is adorned, we are immediately indebted to one body in the countless hosts of space, and that body is the Sun."

It was now 8 a.m. Our good "Fiat" had provided shelter for us for the night, and was now ready for further service.

Rugs were arranged for the ladies' comfort, and we had a good send-off from the house-wife of the Cottage.

We descended the farm hill gently, and were soon one of the perpetual stream of cars returning from Richmond or other places of vantage positions.

We noticed a portion of the road to Darlington was being repaired and re-laid. A large number of men were employed and presented a busy scene. Evidently road repairs in this district was contracted for, because of the quantity of engineering plant and electric devices that were in use for breaking the surface of the old road.

We met with this in several places; also the removing of difficult corners, and cutting new cross-road. We presumed it was all intended for the greater safety of life, and freedom for the car.

We reached Darlington at 8:35 a.m., called at the Police Offices, and were pleased to learn the young man who had fallen from his bike had regained consciousness, and arrangements had been made for his travelling to Newcastle by train. This news gave our ladies, with their tender and womanly hearts, much pleasure.

At Darlington we noticed the electric tram service cars were running on the street without the usual road rails, they were connected with the overhead electric wire.

Our next run was to Newcastle.

When nearing Gateshead we noticed Coal Mines, Factories and Iron Foundries. These industries caused a steady stream of heavy motor lorry traffic.

Coal miners were standing in groups at the corner of streets or open spaces.

The wide street indicated by its surface that it had been well watered during the early morning, and as our car rushed along we could not fail to notice evidence of Coal dust, akin to our Clay dust, which cannot be restrained to a prescribed limit, but demands its freedom with the wind, invading the atmosphere of streets and homes, and leaving its marks and stains. This was very noticeable here.

We left Gateshead for Newcstle by the River, and under a long massive apparently low bridge, but really the high level bridge over the Tyne. A toll was charged.

We then moved slowly along the street. The congestion of traffic would only permit us to travel with the crowd.

Walking on the pavement we noticed a long procession of children, aged from 10 to 14, each carrying a bag or satchel. This procession was under the command of their School teaching staff. We could not fail to note in these children a composure and self reliance, indicating that the rush of street traffic and busy thoroughfares was a part of their every-day life.

These young people, we were informed, were returning home from a hill-side excursion for their viewing the Eclipse. We hoped that these little ones – the men and women of the future – had at least witnessed as much of the Eclipse as we had.

During our short stay here we visited the Forth Engine Motor Works. From the back of this elevated position we had a view of the Tyne. We saw the massive swing bridge; we noticed the busy road on the river-side, the large warehouses, the number of horses employed in haulage work, the Railway bridge crossing the Tyne at a great height so as to admit vessels passing under in their course. Evidently the Architect of this huge structure desired to assist the artist by the graceful architecture employed in its erection. We also noticed the granite was more highly coloured than our Cornish stone.

We left Newcastle at 1:30, and were again in the open and following the tract for Morpeth, arriving there at 2 p.m.

We soon found a Hotel, and were served with a satisfactory lunch.

It was pleasing to hear the company at the other tables chatting with their rythmic voice, an inflection, we thought, that consisted of a mixture of Northumberland, and Scotch border Gaelic.

We noticed this more definitely in the market, or in a broad space used for this purpose. Fruit was very plentiful, Strawberries, Cherries and vegetables in abundance.

We were again on the road at 2-40, with the hope of reaching our destination in the early evening.

Villages appeared more distant from each other here. We passed through a rich pastured valley, so peaceful with its river, and long stretch of trees showing age, irregularly planted with the idea of protecting cattle; the village, too, nestled under the hill. At the extreme end we noticed the village Saddlery.

We called here to enquire the distance to the famous Flodden Battle Field. History tells us that the Flodden Field Battle was fought in the year 1513 between the English and Scots. The Scots were defeated and 10,000 of their Nobles and Army were slain; the English Army was lead by the Earl of Surrey.

The Saddler gave us the impression of being tall, strong, and with the appearance of being a son of the soil. Our question was replied to, we suppose, with his natural mode and dialect expression, such as if we were from America.

We should guess the replies in this wise :—

"How far are we from the Flodden Field ?

"Half a mile up the road opposite the Schoolmaster's house."

"Is there any erection to mark the field ?

"No, not on this road, a cart road leading to the right two miles from the point of the Schoolmaster's house on the brow of the hill, and where the Battle ended, you will find a stone marking the spot."

We thought it was interesting to see a Saddler at work with horses' collars etc., both old and new, on the bench and hanging to pegs.

We suggested it was a farming district, and that the farmers were not using tractors.

His reply came quickly "No", adding "it will be a bad thing when horses are put aside for motors. Horses will have to come back. Farmers know that machines cannot perform the work of the noble horse. Yes the Saddler will always be needed."

We though, when returning to our "Fiat", that our presence here is due to the motor car. He must be a poor tradesman who has no faith in his leather, or what else his occupation might be.

We should enjoy re-producing the difficult mode of expression employed by this native of the lovely valley.

We were again mounting the hill, and attending to our guide's instructions.

The Flodden Fields looked peaceful, the cattle were enjoying its rich pasture.

In view of the valley we were soon at Coldstream, and on the border land of Scotland.

As business men, keen and alert, our petrol tanks were filled here, for we knew over the border we should have to meet an increased charge of 1d. per gallon

We crossed the Bridge, and noticed at the extreme end of its masonry "Scotland".

We said in our minds "Hail, Bonnie Scotland".

It was very pleasing entering Scotland at this point; the road for several miles through pasturages and wooded grounds

We had now come in view of the Cheviot Range, and were looking towards their incincible heights, presenting their undulated and rugged hill-tops.

A powerful Motor Car passed us here, painted Royal Blue. Mrs. George called our attention to this Car as it passed. Had we known its occupants we should have been more alert.

As we ascended the Santra Hill or Pass (its summit reaches 1200 feet) we were met with an expansive view. It was a clear evening, and the pasturage was adorned with the richest green.

The Valleys or Glens, which ran on either side, were clothed in their best, and bright with its spaces of yellow and other shaded flowers.

Our Car was stopped for a time to enjoy the exquisite beauty, and the roughness of the hill-side. In places fences were erected to protect the cattle of the Glen from the dangers of heights and overhanging ledges, which apparently had little soil covering and little pasture.

These hill-tops and crags shewed the Glens in a very artictis form, the whole effect of light and shade and colour seeming to create a beautifully woven carpet.

We were all thrilled at our experience, and drank deeply of the Zephyrs ladened with perfumes from mountain and glen.

Our thoughts travelled back to the time of the Covenantors who were hunted to judgment, and to death, by Claverhouse and his men.

These noble Scotsmen stood the test at this period for liberty of conscience in their worship and service to God.

We have often thought how these noble men of character could have hidden from the terrors that surrounded them.

This elevated Pass, with its uninterrupted view, gave us he answer, which was confirmed later in our travel.

We realised that Scotland was the land of Mountains and Glens, Lakes, Islands and rivers, and held tracts of rough unproductive spaces, which would provide scope for hiding and cover. As we left the freshness of the hill and descended to the plain, continuing our journey toward Dalkeith, the Road for quite a distance was in bad condition with pot-holes. Mr. George used the alertness of the skilful driver while on this patch.

From the start Mr. George was cognisant of the preciousness of his charge, and his kindly thought was for safety and comfort.

We passed apparently miles of moorland, the roads or moors were protected by wire fencing. No doubt this would be the home of the Crofter, and his sheep pasturage.

As we neared Dalkeith, from the Hill, we caught a glimpse of Edinburgh in the distance.

In passing through the small towns of Scotland we were met with notice boards informing motorists that they must not esceed 15 miles per hour through the town. We wondered if these notices were effective. Many cars passed us going through these towns travelling at a speed much in advance of the stated limit.

On the next hill after passing Dalkeith we had a fine view of Edinburgh. In its beauty and splendour it appeared to us a fairy City; the Castle in its impregnable form; Arthur's seat at its back with the grey hale or sheen reaching up to meet the clouds, and its steeples and imposing buildings.

This momentary glimpse sped us on to reach the Imperial City of Scotland.

We entered the suburbs of the City about 6:15 p.m. The streets with the 3 and 4 storied houses gave us the impression of a University, or Professional character.

We followed the tram line which led us to Princes Street, which is regarded as one of the most beautiful boulevards of the World.

Our "Fiat" with her 9 horse power propelling her burden of, may we say, travellers with the pride of Crofters in their hearts, seeking romance – the romance that Edinburgh and her people advertise to the World.

In our route we passed the Caledonian Hotel and Railway Station, on our right also the Castle and Gardens.

At the Waverley Hotel and station we turned to our left for George Street and our Hotel.

We were greeted soon after our arrival by Miss Harris, and who can measure the thrill of joy it gave to Sisters and Brother, and in which we as new friends had a share.

It is a great blessing to feel the affinity of friendship, and to know one is breathing the same atmosphere of the lone place, or City, as a friend.

This thought of itself is a real comfort in discarding lonliness, and of un-assessed value in promoting confidence.

After rest we joined our friends at dinner. The waiter, with his experience of travellers and Globetrotters, assumed we had travelled from a distance, and soon detected that we were not from the Hills, Glens or Islands of Scotland.

How often, when we are conversation with strangers may-be from East, West, North or South, we had wondered why we do not all speak the words as written; we have a common literature which directs the thoughts in a common language.

Our conversation here was directed mainly by the visitors to the visitor, who was very interested in our journey.

LOCH LOMOND AND
BEN LOMOND

LUSS AND BEN LOMOND

LUSS STRAIGHTS

ROB ROYS PRISON

MARRIAGE AT GRETNA GREEN

We soon discovered that beside the kindly thought and attention for our comfort, we had met a guide who possessed a very comprehensive knowledge of Scotland, and its places of historic interest.

After our meal we decided to have a walk. It was a pleasant evening, and the light had not yet faded, and we were anxious to see Princess Street in its evening architectural beauty, and listen to the Gaelic notes of its throngs and look down ovwe its City garden or park, apparently presided over by the monument to Sir Walter Scott, and as the steady rush of tram and car passed us on both ways we looked at massive business houses and shops, with names of Scotch proprietorship or Limited Companies, that of itself conveyed a lesson Geography.

As we returned to the George Hotel feeling refreshed by our interesting walk, we with out best wishes bade each other good-night and returned to our rooms for rest, with this reflection in our minds, the difference as between the City street and the quiet Country roads.

"Our first morning in Edinburgh" came to us with our waking thoughts. We also had the feeling of freshness, and remembered we were units of a City with a population of over 420,000 souls, and in a City inseparably associated with the history, more especiall of Mary Queen of Scots, also of the author of the Waverley Novels, of which he so proudly referred to in "Marmion".

"Mine own Romantic Town".

We did not forget the pleasant walk of the previous evening as we travelled the entirelength of Princess Street, and visited the famour Floral Clock.

This is one of the City's commanding attractions, with its movement of Floral hands, its figures of flowers, each in separate shades, and the fancy patchwork of cultivated flowers and mosses of differenc colours, and looking so beautifully fresh as the revolving hands so quietly pointed to the correct time, with a staeliness that was equal to the clock set in Tower or Observatory.

As we followed the interests of the Street we were constantly reminded that Edinburgh possessed both heart and soul, and that her citizens delighted to honour her illustrious sons, who had contributed both to National and International wheal, and reforming influences, and as we looked at the ststue of David Livingstone of African fame, of Dr. Guthrie the famous orator, Divine, and leader of thought, of Sir James Y.Simpson, the discoverer of chloroform which has done so much for the alleviation of pain, and brought a new era of confidence and hope to the inmates of the Wards and consulting rooms of our noble institutions.

We also saw other commemorating statues, adding distinction, and displaying the work of the sculptor in its beauty, portraying noble faces, and giving the residents and visitors ideals, and noble resolutions, and as we looked gown across the gardens or pleasure grounds, and then scanned the romantic Castle with the twilight gently enveloping its heights, and gradually surrounding its rocks and craigs, we thought "Yes, it is very beautiful, and no mean thing to "be numbered with this City in its population."

Whilst we thus mused there were other pleasures to be thought of.

We were all anxious to give every hour its true value and as we sat around the breakfast table laid for four, with its Scotch appetising fare, our position gave us an out-look on to the wide street with its high and broad windows.

The Commercial element of the room was very evident as we noticed the keen faces, and their absorption of the daily Newspapers.

As we enjoyed the provision from the table, and the little humours directed at us from our Ladies, it was a question as to which gave us the most pleasure. Yes, breakfast was necessary, for we were contemplating our programme for the day, but what a cold existence life would be without its humour, especially when conceived in well and true balanced minds.

The conclusion to our discussion was made on a definite line; that we would do our utmost to make this visit to Edinburgh one of permanent thought to memory, and with this as our standard we commenced our tour of the City.

The first item on the programme was to visit the Forth Bridge. Accordingly we took the tram for the Caledonian Hotel terminus, and then by Char-abanc. We secured our seats near the Conductor, and with our usual friendly tone asked him to point to us places of interest on the route, which he assured us, would be his pleasure.

When passing over the Forth Bridge – a fine structure – we were informed it was 100 feet high. We presumed that we were passing over what was in the very early days a Glen, which led even then into the famous City.

Our attention was next directed to the ancient Gammon Brig, built by the Romans and still in public use, also large apparently public buildings en route.

As we emerged from the busy thoroughfares into the quieter or less busy part we could hear our Mr. George, who by this time had gained the Conductor's genial laugh, plying him with as what we can readily understand, Cornish twit, or joke.

The following were a few of the questions addressed to him:—

"Is it true that you do not allow the Cocks to crow on Sundays"?

Is it true that your Oatmeal and Oat Cakes are indispensible in your daily diet?"

Is it true that Haggis is the most favoured dish to a Scotsman?"

Is it true that you could not exist without your shortbread?"

These were the outline of questions which provided the hearty laughter and gay pleasure to our company.

Passing on the now country road we were shown a path that led us a steep hill both difficult and long, at the end of which was a seat with the inscription "Rest and be thankful".

We next came to a view of the Dalmenly Estate, which extended to the banks of the Forth. Our Conductor informed us that Lord Roseberry was expected in residence during the week. We thought by the respectful tones and references that Lord Roseberry was regarded in high esteem.

We next had a view of workings similar to our Cornish Mines, with its burrows of refuse, and were informed that these were Shale Mines from which Petroleum Oil was extracted.

Descending the hill we had a magnificent view of the Firth of Forth Bridge.

We alighted from the bus, and walked a distance to gain, if possible, a clearer view and better estimate of its magnitude and length.

Fog, or a low lying mist, prevented us at first from tracing the gigantic structure to the opposite side at Queensferry.

During our wait we became friendly with the River men, who in conversation gave us information about its construction, the difficulties of the Engineers, the number of men employed, the difficulties of the workers and their capabilities.

Apparently this Bridge is over a mile long, has one natural support – the Ingarvia Island – half way across. Its cost was over £3,000,000 and took seven years to build. It was opened to traffic by King Edward VIII in the year 1890.

These men also pointed to the bend of the River, and informed us that within the bend was Rosyth Naval Base.

A steam ferry still plies from the pier on the South Queenferry side.

We were interested here, and could easily compare the Ferry landling to one of our Cornish Fair or Feast Fields with its number of stalls for the sale of fruit, toys and the endless other ware.

While we were awaiting the return of the Bus we noticed several trains pass over the Bridge, and calculated that each were five minutes in crossing.

Before we left the fog lifted. We thought this compensated us for our wait.

We could now trace the opposite shore.

Our visit to this World-wide-known famous Bridge demanded of us more than a casual survey, hence our thought of this immense structure reminded us that here was a pile of nature's resources. The massive granite pillars reared from deep down through water and mud to the firm foundation of natural rock. The immense crescent formed Arches reared skyward, with practically numberless iron girdirs, frames, stays and bolts, and required labour, skilled and practical to complete it.

Is there not the first cause also, when we think of its conception; the intense and wide range of thought of the Architect centred in plan and specification with its minute detail for its strength, rigidity and the principle of safety. He remembered it was for this and future generations.

The spanning of this great river of commerce linking up the North and South, gave speed and safety to travel.

Here we can see the advance of civilized thought as between the crossing in the vigorous winter by Ferry-boat, and the heated comfortable carriage that now carries one over the Bridge to the Cities and Towns of the North.

We rejoined the Bus for the return journey, and had the pleasure of viewing the landscapes and varied scenic beauties and fertility of the County from the opposite point of the compass to our outward travel.

The Car, we thought, was employed in useful service in conveying passengers from the outlying districts to their Metropolis.

Our interest was attracted to a vivacious girl; her merry mood and pleasant chat to her friends gave pleasure to the Company.

We had not noticed the quality of dourness so often attributed to the thoughtful Scotsman, but their pleasantries in the vernacular were both pleasing and instructive.

We met Miss Harris on our return, who with her constant kindness had arranged a visit to one of the large general businesses.

This interested us, and gave us an idea of a City business, and what it supplies to the community, stocks of goods wherever one looked – reaching from floor to ceiling, the premises so lavishly furnished with Stands, Cases, and Mirrors; the massive pillars embellished with artistic thought and utilised for the display of beautiful goods.

We thought of this as on the lines of the great London shops, such as Barkers or Selfridges.

The assistant, too, used tact with business acumen.

Inspectors, or Showroom Managers, were standing or moving around at the siair entrance or corridors, each with the dignity and appearance of proprietorship.

Our progress led us to the spacious Dining Hall, in which our guide and hostess had ordered Lunch.

Our conversation whilst at the meal was both general and reflective, and had its bearing on our quest of the morning, and our impression of the various departments of the house we had passed through.

We dare not compare our own little modest concern with this spacious market, so replete in the adaptation of the complete requirements of Edinburgh and its visiting public – imagination, too, compelled attention. Presumably this business had been built to its present success by the intuitive and mental power of men who had given a great portion of time and energy to its progress.

May not these successful business men be classified with, say, the Engineers of the Forth Bridge, or other famous men who have gained distinction by constructive work in the realm of public service; all have used their gifts, and probably their greatest powers in building and developing in the various sphers for the requirements and ever-needy public.

The time we spent here was regarded with great pleasure, and, we think, enlarged our business thoughts and standards.

Our hostess gave us a good time.

At 2-30 we were on the busy street again, wending our way to the picturesque Castle, Edinburgh's traditional stronghold.

History reminds us that a Fortress was built on this rock in A.D. 633, by Edwin the Anglian King of Northumbria.

What revelations are handed down to us by historical records, and is it not a fact that only the noble in heart and life, who have been courageous for National ideals and rendered service worthy of commendation, have been made the stars of history.

33

As we walked up the Hill leading to the Castle, and gazed on its impregnable rocks, so firm and stable that buildings have been erected on its very edge, and as we entered its precincts its stone paved road led us to its main archway entrance to the Castle.

If these stones could tell their story, what a history it would unfold of the Armies and various classes of nobles and peoples who have trod these echoing stone pavements.

We may think of Kings and Queens, Statesmens and Nobles who have distinguished themselves in the realm of courageous actions, and citizens and soldiers who for love of Country have dares for the rights or wrongs of leadership.

We joined a party who were being escorted by an official guide. This guide pointed out the positions of the four gates that in early days gave entrance to the stronghold.

The protection walls were very thick, with warrior look-outs at vantage positions.

On the ramparts Mors Meg was in position. This huge and famous piece of Ordnance was used in the seige of Dumbarton in 1489. This cannon is said to be one of the first used, and shows by its twisted bands evidences of its exploding.

We next visited the old State Prison. Our guide informed us that many Nobles, including the two Argylls, had been imprisoned here before their execution.

We were also conducted to the chamber in which Queen Mary gave birth to James VI; also to the Regalia Chamber or Crown Room, in which are deposited the Scottish Regalia, exhibited in a similar manner as the Crown Jewels in the Tower of London.

Within a massive glass case, with other relics, may be seen the Crown of Robert Bruce.

The Caretaker here gave us a very detailed reply to our enquiries.

One of our party was taking notes of dates etc. and was immediately requested to desist, as often exaggerated reports, not containing exactness, had appeared in Newspapers and reports, especially on the other side of the Atlantic. Our friend replied that they were simply aids to memory, and for private use.

A huge oak chest, studded with bolts and screws, was shown us, in which the Jewels had been stored and protected before and during the Great War.

We next visited what was considered to be the oldest building within the Castle Close, the St.Margaret's Chapel, a very small room as we consider Churches.

We next visited the ancient Scotch Parliament Hall, containing a mass of National relics, and contrasts, from the first of ancient guns to the modern rifle, coats-of-arms, massive spears and battle-axes and choice carvings.

One longed for a memory which would contain the half of what was seen here, nay a small percentage of the Exhibition wherein was stored, may we say the Faith and Strength of Scotland's past.

In the Royal Palace Court was erected the Scottish National War Memorial. This presents a work of art. It was to be unveiled by the Prince of Wales on a day in the following week.

Royalty were making their annual visit to Holyrood Palace.

This is apparently a great occasion, preparations are made on a regal scale as a royal welcome.

As we left the Castle, we saw on each side of the broad Courtyard memorials erected to Naval and Army Commanders or Generals who had held victorious commands.

A very interesting incident met us here. Two little boys, presumably not above the age of 10 years, we thought with courage offered their services as guides, and commenced to point to each memorial, giving date, name of battle and the history of the encounter, taking each here in turn.

Their voices sounded in unison, their hands in pointing to their subjects, and pauses, were as clock-work, and gave us childish eloquence.

After rewarding them, and in reply to our enquiry we were told that what we had listened to had been taught them from the official Guide, and presumably for helping Mother in the household expenses.

In returning from the Castle at 5:15 p.m. we passed the old Gabled house in which John Knox the great reformer lived and died, and which now contains his chair and other relics.

In passing up the street, and near St. Giles Cathedral, we were accosted by a Cabby who pressed us to engage him for a fare to any of the interesting parts of the City or environs.

JOHN RUSKIN, CRITIC AND AUTHOR

AMBLESIDE AND WANSFELL

FITZ PARK

FITZ PARK AND KESWICK HOTEL

MAIN STREET AND TOWN HALL, KESWICK

KESWICK AND DERWENTWATER

In pressing his services with a flow of cabby language he stated he had been a cab-man for 40 years, and knew the City and every spot that would be of interest to visitors.

From our observation we thought the passing of the Cab in Edinburgh was almost complete, and this solitary Cab was one of the last to tell the tale and remind us of their glorious past, and of their usefullness to the needy as a public convenience.

In this case we were faced with the passing of the great and glorious past, which will soon become history. Even this change has become an actual fact during the last decade.

Well we may pause as we hear or read of mechanical and other sciences that are occupying the mind and study of the men of super intellect. The laboratories are unfolding many secrets, and as mind and matter are investigating the mighty atom which is so powerful, and whithholds its secret and forbids to have its powers wrenched except by strenous mental thought, who can doubt but that the finite mind is led by the infinite power of the Unseen in the discovery of the marvellous powers for the progress of civilization.

Many deplore the passing of the Cab, and many welcome the Petrol or Electric spark.

In the meantime we wait for the advent of the harnessing of other and mightier forces which will be claimed in service for the world's advancement and its Utopian future.

We returned to George Street for tea, and discussed our programme for the morrow.

We all thought that a trip on the Lakes, and through the Trossacks should be taken, and the evening was occupied by our friends who decided to visit the suburbs of the City, and ourselves would see the evening pictures as exhibited by the City streets.

Leaving the Hotel and walking Northward we were attracted by a Church, and whilst reading the Notices the Minister came to us and gave us a warm welcome to visit the Church, saying this was the St. Andrew's Church which was the scene of the epoch making disruption in 1843.

In conversation I called him by name; he immediately enquired, being a stranger, how I knew his name as Dr. Christie. We could easily satisfy him on this point as we had previously seen his name on the Notice of Public Service.

We also thought we knew him by repute. We thought he had appeared on the B.W.

The Minister, a tall, well proportioned gentleman, with a pleasing smile, gave us a very interesting time.

We entered the Church. It was quite round, and every seat was arranged that the Minister and congregation confronted each other.

We next came to a wide street crossing, and in the centre of the wide space was a beautiful memorial to W. Ewart Gladstone. The design displayed in a wonderful way the emblems or characteristics that this great Christian Statesman recognised as the only bases on which laws relating to Nations, communities, industrial and individual life could be founded and hope to attain success.

We thought this was one of the most beautiful statues of the many that practically confront the visitor at every open space.

We were also interested in a very high Column, similar to Nelson's column in London. This was erected in a public garden enclosure, but as the light was fading we were unable to trace to whom this memorial was erected.

We made courses for Princess Street. Who has not heard of Scotch mist?

At first we thought the elements were unkind to us. We opened our umbrellas for protection against the light thick rain. As we soon became a part of the Princess Street crowd we assented to the thought of Safety First, rather than risk the danger of our umbrella wires on the passing crowd, and used our gamps as walking sticks.

As the crowds were hurrying to their various destinations we thought what a democratic principle the rain employs. It falls on all alike, both quality and quantity, feathers and flowers, silks and cottons, and that without respect to person or position. Yet how dependent human nature is on the health giving mercies of the crystal drops of rain, with its health giving influence on forest and field, and gardens, Rivers and Lakes, and even in the flushing and cleansing of our sewage systems.

Our next experience presented a very sad picture, showing that this great City and population were not under prohibition law. Who could not feel sorrowful for this young girl that was hurred past in charge of two Policemen in a state of alcoholic collapse, being practically carried, her head thrown back with dazed appearance and senses bedimmed. She had sacrificed her will power to alcohol.

Yes, this was the saddest scene we witness on our journey.

We next determined to make our way to Holyrood Palace, and in order to gain shelter and proceed quickly we were directed to a tram that ran near the Palace. Practically every seat on the tram was occupied. On the point of starting an aged lady entered. Immediately a kindly girl offered her seat, which was accepted – the girl standing. In studying the features of the girl we concluded that this kindly act gave her much pleasure.

We were informed by the Conductor that we had now arrived at the street nearest to our objective. As we alighted this girl also left the tram, and in reply to question we addressed to her as to the turning at the Cross streets she immediately offered her services as guide.

We thanked her, reminding her it was raining and she would probably be needed at home. She graciously put our excuses aside, and said the rain did not matter, that she was not expected home so early and assured us it would be a pleasure to her.

As we listened to the pleasant voice of our girl guide, the walk became more pleasant.

We soon noticed that she knew the history of "Mine own Town"; each Street held its romance and the name of the street was not casually given.

Royalty and famous men were remembered in this part of Edinburgh in the naming of streets and houses.

We were soon at the Palace.

History states it was completed for the reception of James II and VII, and his family in 1679. Adjoining apparently a part of the Palace is the Abbey, founded by David I and heralded as one of the great religious houses of Scotland, and had offered asylum to many great and faithful men.

For many years the place was used as right of sanctuary, and was used as such, till recent year. A well defined line in the pavement still marks the place within which fugitives were safe from arrest.

The Palace is very imposing with its turretted walls and massive appearance – the home and fortress of Kings and Queens.

The entrance is protected with very interesting – apparently hand forged – iron railings.

In the centre or main entrance to the Palace is a very fine example of granite in a monument to King Edward VII.

We noticed that the Abbey was in a state of ruin, with only the walls standing.

Our little guide was well adapted to her task, and we were next taken to the famous St. Margaret's Wishing Well, and to a point where we had a good view of Arthur's Seat, and the park or ground in which Volunteer reviews etc. used to be held.

We should have liked to have been in time to have entered the Palace, but were informed that it was closed from that day in order to prepare the state rooms for Royalty which were due the following week.

As we returned to the tram and our hotel the walk was very interesting. Our guide's conversation did not cease, and was a source of pleasure and information.

Many houses and places were pointed out to us which gave us the impression that every stone and spot held secrets of history and romance.

Our little guide's name and address was requested. With reluctance she wrote on our note book, but looking at it later we presumed her modesty would not admit of her giving her name, but the name of the street only.

We returned to our Hotel and awaited the return of Mr. & Mrs George. We enjoyed a pleasant hour in the spacious Drawing Room of the Hotel, to which many of the tourists resorted in order to meet their friends, and recount the experiences of the day.

We thought these pleasant mutual meeting of the intimate friendships resembled or provided opportunities for thought and conversation, as often in our Country rambles we choose our subject and invariably receive helpful and vivifying thought, or we may implant helpful suggestions or ideas to our friend or companion.

We decided to retire early, and be mindful of the time arranged for to-morrow's journey and pleasure.

We were astir early, and were with the first to enter the Dining Room for breakfast.

Our train was due to leave the Caledonian Station at 8:30 a.am.

We chatted at the breakfast table on the question of our enterprising trip, which would take us over historical country, famous for legendary and imaginary plots, which Scott has shown us in vivid incidents.

Arriving at the Station in good time, we secured our tickets for Balloch via Glasgow.

From the carriage window one gets a glimpse of the passing show. As the train proceeded to Glasgow we had a view of busy streets, large ware-houses, engineering works and foundries.

After leaving the border towns of Edinburgh the country appeared to be very sparsely populated. The field and lands generally gave us the impression of being well cultivated. Cattle and stock did not show as plentiful as in our South part of England.

As the train sped forward we also had time for reverie; the thick mist we had started with had turned to rain and the thought of this suggested the question "Are we justified in taking this trip to the Lakes and through the Trossacks?" Then our second thought came as a flash.

"This was our only opportunity" which thought gave notice to the doubt, and furnished us with minds that were willing to "do and dare".

As we neared Glasgow, Scotland's Metropolis of Industry with its population of 1,034,069, the conversation of our young lady guide of the previous evening asserted itself "Yes, Edinburgh and Glasgow are not considered the same, the difference is that Edinburgh people are reserved and more on professional or university lines, while Glasgow people are more free and frank, and always anxious to be of service or show kindness to the stranger".

With this thought we welcomed our approach to the great commercial city of the Clyde.

It was raining heavily when we reached Glasgow high level platform. Our first thought was "What a huge station with so many platforms, and at different angles."

The ticket collector informed us we had an hour to wait for the Balloch train.

We were anxious to have a view of the Clyde, if only to see where and how our imported China Clay and China Stone cargoes were discharged, but the rain was relentless, and it became us to be prudent. We were strangers in a strange land, and to risk getting wet might have occasioned circumstances not to our comfort or advantage.

We did venture under our Umbrellas through a very busy street. It was very apparent to us that Glasgow people were smart in their walk and movements. Rain had little influence on them; they appeared to rely on their raincoats for protection.

The street here was wide, but only capable of providing space and moving room for the tremendous number of vehicles that were travelling with their burden or merchandise each way.

The shops, to a Country Trader, were marvellous from various aspects. May we say first that cleanliness was very apparent. Assistants were attired in clean white coats, counters were attractive with burnished scale, and the mahogany polished windows appeared as if an Artist had been at work so decorative and alluring were the goods placed, and so attractive to the passing public and purchaser.

We thought we had seen but little of this mighty Glasgow, with its famous Cathedral, its University, its Municipal Buildings and Public Parks, its shipbuilding for all Nations, its manufacture of machinery and products, its imports and exports, not forgetting our own industry of Mid-Cornwall to assist their industries of Pottery, bleaching and the material for their compositions, and we would not except the political strenuousness of their Politics as shown by their Representatives at St. Stephens.

The hour quickly passed. We enjoyed the moving picture of this vast human tide as it ebbed and flowed from the shelter under the massive Railway Arch, with its realistic market, or covered street, of shops. The electric globes giving light from the Shops which formed a part of the Arch gave it a fairy-like appearance, and so varied were the wares that one could purchase jewellery, outfitting, furniture, provisions, fruits or confections; in fact everything that is required, or appeal to one's fancy.

We returned to the lower level platform, & secured a comfortable carriage.

What we had seen during the morning quickened our interest, and as the train moved out of the station we were rewarded with a fine view of the Riverside, revealing the fact that here was a hive of industry. Shipbuilding yards showed ships in various stages of construction. Many Yards of celebrated firms reached for a great distance. There were mechanical works, and factories, apparently without number.

The dwelling-houses gave us the impression of being well constructed on the "Flats" system. We thought how very tedious it must be for the heads of families living on the 3rd or 4th floor. We thought we should not appreciate change from our quiet and pleasant district to those crowded streets and houses.

Our window presented us with very fine scenery of the Zig-Zag course of the River and the opposite banks. We passed Clydebank, Dumbarton and other stations with their Scotch, but familiar names.

It occupied about an hour in travel from Glasgow to Ballock Pier Station, and every mile gave us interest and pleasure and wonder, as we viewed things on the larger scale.

As the train sped on we had only a peep of old Castles and Mansions, which no doubt could provide a book of history, of clans and people.

From Dumbarton we commenced our ascent until we reached the Pier.

We think the famous Loch Lomond is about 400 feet above the Clyde level.

At Balloch the traveller crosses the platform to the waiting Steamer.

We noticed a party of American tourists, who had travelled from Glasgow, crossing the platform, and like us, were embarking for a trip in the miniature Liner on the Scotch Loch-Atlantic voyage.
The Captain looked every inch a Sailor with brass buttons and rimmed cap.
Positions were selected and the Liner's propellor was started on its revolving duty.

The seamen were ship-shape in coiling their mooring ropes on deck, and aware we had started our journey and were steaming pleasantly on the smooth water of what has been termed the Queen of Scottish Lakes.

We now had an opportunity of quietly surveying the district, and the scenery on the banks of the Loch.

The weather was now beautifully fine.

Human nature is both difficult to define or satisfy hence we were thankful the rain had cleared but we wanted just sufficient wind to separate and drive the clouds so as to admit the glorious sunshine.

We wanted to see the effect on the peaceful water of the alternate cloud and sunlight reflections of the wooded Islands and Mountains, and of the continuous weather beaten rocks reaching skyward as a challenge to their King, Ben Lomond, whose towering height could be seen from all points.

On the West side of the Loch trees with rich foliage lined its banks. Mansions and Castles could be located at various commanding points, and rising at the back of this level were the eternal hills, so that from each side these high and rugged peaks formed a body-guard to the peaceful Loch.

Sitting near us on the deck of our Liner were two ladies who conversed in Gaelic. Both possessed rich toned voices. We could not understand their conversation, but we enjoyed the flexible tone of their voices as we would the harmony of music.

Passing the first Island we enquired of these ladies its name, and if inhabited. We were informed its Gaelic name, and then its English meaning as "Island of the Monks" or "Nuns' Island". Apparently there was formerly a Monastry on the Island. No doubt this Island has a history charged with romance.

Our first Port or landing stage was Balmatia. I think we regretted our two Gaelic ladies landing here.

Our next stopping place was Lass. We now came in full view of Ben Lomond. At first it appeared grey and barren. As we approached it we could see a narrow white line running a Zig-Zag course.

As we neared it became larger, showing itself a stream of water gathering quantity and power in its descent to the Loch.

We also noticed that instead of grey surroundings, vegetation and grass grew on its slopes and to its crown.

We were now nearing our landing Pier as Inversnaid, and could see Coaches and men standing by dressed in Red Coats, and black velvel hats.

42

MOTORING THROUGH LAKELAND
DUNMAIL RAISE

HONISTER PASS

FALCON CRAGG

DERWENTWATER

THIRLMERE AND HELVELLYN

WATERHEAD AND WINDERMERE LAKE

GRASMERE CHURCH

THIRLMERE AND HELVELLYN

SEEING BRITAIN FIRST.- A girl climber bent on conquering
steep and risky slopes in the Lake District. There is no more
popular district in England for more adventurous rambler.

RUSKINS MONUMENT

We later had the pleasure of riding behind these old-world dressed coachmen in their springless four-in-hand coaches.

Our trip on the Loch occupied about 13/4 hours.

We enjoyed the Lunch served on the boat, consisting of purely Scotch food, and salmon caught from the Loch.

The Liner after landing us preceeded on her voyage to the far end of the Loch.

We thought a person or guide should be appointed to point out the many places of interest, both on the Loch and on the trip; tourists would gladly pay the extra cost.

We were a good company to leave the boat here. The Coaches were ready to take us to Loch Katrine.

The four horses in each Coach knew their duties, where to stop, and when to gallop, apparently trained so as to give effective glamour to the trip. (Lest we forget, from enquiries we find the Loch Lomond is 22 miles in length, 3/4 miles in breadth at the upper end and 5 miles at the lower, and the depth is from 6 to 630 feet).

The road to Loch Katrine led us up the Mountain side – a road rough and unsteady. A river from the mountain had cut a ravine on our right, and sang in great frollicing merriment as it rushed on its course to join the Loch below.

Trees grew on either side.

When nearing the summit of the hill we passed the Farm house known as the Garrison.

Looking back, and at the other side of the valley, the mountain scene was entrancing.

We were near Ben Lomond. On the opposite side was Ben Ime, 3,319 feet, and away on the North Ben Vorlich 3092 feet.

As we gained the summit the road led us under the shadow of high rocks. Here we passed a farm or Crofter's house. Cultivated land? No, as far as the eye could reach hill-tops and barreh-ness; a mountain waste without trees.

We now came to Loch Arklet, which supplies Glasgow with her pure water – 34 miles distant.

From here our coaches increased their speed on the running ground; this without extra comfort to the passengers, as one can well believe on is riding in a trade cart.

At Stronachlachar we embarked in the "Sir Walter Scott" for our trip on Loch Katrine. The afternoon was very pleasant, and we again enjoyed the 10 miles trip to the Trossacks Pier.

Post Cards were on sale on board the boat.

On the left side of the lake several large houses were well placed in park-like grounds.

On the other side it was bounded by the peaks of the high and mountainous district, with Ben Aun and on the right Ben Venue, and looking ahead towards the Trossacks, Ben Lede.

It was all so fairy-like being propelled on the smooth clean water.

We missed the smell of salt and sea-weed, and the pure ozone of the ocean, but even here were compensations with the Mountain, Valley and Loch health-giving elixer, coming from the far North in its purity and strength.

We noticed that on this Loch a masonry wall was being built around it so as to increase its capacity.

The Trossacks Piere is very quaint. The steamer brings one round an Island to the mountain-side Pier, laid out with rustic charm, and a wood-land retreat.

We were met here with Motor-Cars and conveyed to the Trossacks Hotel for tea.

On this occasion we decided to remain with the car. The sun was shining with vigour and the district was very beautiful with Loch, woodland, terraced rocks, and not least, our mutual companionship, so that our half hour's rest was enjoyed to the full.

At the appointed time we were required to be seated for our journey to Callender Station.

Our American contingent had kept very severely to themselves, and apparently quite satisfied with their own particular company.

It happened that in our Car we were favoured to have the seat between Mr. George and myself allotted to an American lady. We at first failed to get her in conversation, but on addressing the following question to her the restraint was broken; the question was "How do you Americans know of "the Historic places of England"? "How do we know?" was the reply, "Do we not read your books, the Waverley Novels, Shakespeare, Dickens and your other books of History, they have a place in all American Libraries, and are read and studied as our own; hence we are anxious to cross the Atlantic and visit the places and scenes that have been so naturally and vividly portrayed by Historian and Author."

We enjoyed her conversation. Her American accent was dropped, and we all had real pleasure from her interesting conversation.

The drive from the Trossacks is almost indescribable, so varied was the scenery of mountain heights and deep valleys, of its moss covered rocks, which at places ever-hung the road, and purple heather filled the spaces between the huge rocks.

Here, we thought, is Nature at its best, its wildness and its beauty so blended to make the setting harmonious and as our Coach proceeded and we scanned the Mountainous height, its stern and rugged summit, and then as we had a glimpse of the trees growing upward to the height on the opposite side, one could but think "Yes, this is a picture "of Nature's grandeur, and what we witnessed & enjoyed that day will make us happy in the memory of our short visit to that district.

We thus give our impressions of our days trip after allighting at Callendar Railway Station.

We had an hour to wait for our train and the time was pleasingly engaged in viewing the outline of the surrounding district, which to us seemed so full of interest.

At the rear of the station, which was approached from the North by a tunnel, the rugged rocks ran to precipitious heights, with trees in the sheltered hollows, and higher up short stubby growths with furze which gave the colour of its bloom, and mingling with the jutting rocks revealing gaiety to the outline of the mountainous peaks. On the right of the station was a small loch with a belt of trees dressed in their early July green, and another to the East of the small Town, which, on looking in that direction, appeared on a level with a distant ridge of hills. This would be the ideal home of the Crofter and Sportsman.

After leaving the car, our American friends again linked up with their travelling companions, which was practically good life to us. We further noticed, when the train slowed to the platform that they told the Guard 'We are Cooks, first class'.

The wait passed very pleasently, and we enjoyed tea from the Railway Refreshment Saloon. We thought the Ladies in charge were interested in us and presume it was the little member who gave 'we away', but if we had crossed the Atlantic and had spoken in sharp guessing sentences we could not have had better attention shewn us. On reflection, it is wonderful what the coin stands for. Its commanding influence cannot be fully estimated even in its tender for the refreshing cups of tea. We had their thanks in Gaelic sweetness, thus conveying pleasure and gratitude. It is obvious to the traveller that one must be provided with the necessary. Its a clever person that can travel the highways without this element that makes for the World's progress and provides for International exchange, thus giving confidence and good understanding, and what applies to Nations applies also to individuals and communities, the basis of elementary and natural life. We read of Domestic and Political economy and we think of the Economist as one prudent in expenditure, but limitation often acts as a detterent and claims attention.

We had now a train journey of 60 miles to Edinburgh, which for the time being we regarded as home. We should have enjoyed a travelling friend who could have pointed out, and given us the names of Turreted Castles and strongholds of the Scottish Clans, and told us of what renown or special interest was attached to these places as our train hurried along to keep her scheduled time.

On looking through the carriage window, we presumed, by the names of the stations, that we saw the famous Wallace Memorial the Battle field of Bannockburn, Hirling Castle and other places probably of equal interest. We had hoped that our train would have returned via the Firth of Forth bridge, but apparently this was not in the Railway Route, as our train entered the suburbs of Edinbourgh we noticed various works and stores representing the commercial activities of the City. We arrived at Calledonia Station at 7 p.m.

As we returned to our Hotel, we reminded ourselves that we had had a long day of travelling, and the constant stream of traffic, Motors, busses and crowd of pedestrians demanded both wit and care, and did not permit soliloquising on the busy streets.

We were glad to get to the Hotel if only to satisfy the craving of a Scottish appetite, or what is often expressed in Cornwall as "wanting a cup of tea".

The table for four was laid attractively for keen appetites, and half an hour gave satisfying results, each of us expressed ourselves, that although we had had a long day and travelled a long distance, neither complained of fatigue. Our conversation led us to the fact that the following morning we should, with regret, bid adieu to Edinburgh and make our trek for "down along and home along".

Our Ladies thought it best to do the packing, while Mr. George and myself decided for a walk. We followed George Street to the corner, and we were anxious to again visit the Gladstone Memorial. We expressed ourselves as to the Sculptor's achievement in depicting Greatness in this memorial of Granite and Bronze, reminding the City and all that pass by, the grandeur of devoting the God given gifts with a quenchless encroy, and working on an imagination of what the British Empire could attain to, and the course that political action and life should follow. Hence the Statesman honoured by all Nationally and Politically being dead yet speaketh in History to present and future Parliaments of the Worlds. We next looked at the massive pillars that gives St. Andrews Church such fame and impressive appearance. We next went on to Princess Street. The Natural light was now giving place to twilight and the Electric bulb. As we looked towards the Waverley Hotel and Station (we were near the Scotts memorial) we halted a few moments in reverie. From this position we had a view of the Colton Hill with its National monuments, Columbs, City observatory and other memorials of equal fame. On turning gently to the right and tracing the skyline, we noticed the dim light from many windows, we could see the towering height of Arthur Seat (822 feet), and then the Castle on the nearest height. It appeared as if the gardens stretching down the valley and then upward to the Castle. We could also see a part of old Edinburgh nestled further up the valley, with its busy streets and congested population, thus in a few minutes we were rewarded with the beauty of the City's outline in the shadows of the changing light. We could not even then restrain the thought that we should be leaving this entrancing City on the morrow. We again crossed Princess Street, with its midway protections for the safety of the Pedestrian in crossing. We think the City Street Authorities should be complimented in their thoughtful provision for 'Public Safety'.

We were soon back to the Hotel and decided to retire for rest and renewal of the forces that one needs for fitness and the power of enjoying the complex blessing of the senses both common and others, that is derived from the unseen source which comes so mysteriously by natures healer – SLEEP. What better example can we have than that of the child – Evenings or bed-time tired and peavish – Mornings bright and happy, ready for the new day.

The following morning at 8.15 a.m. we met at the Breakfast table, our waiter greeting us with his genial smile. During the meal we enquired of our waiter 'To whom was the memorial and the tall column dedicated' (we had previously referred to this memorial). He replied somewhat in this manner – 'He could not give the name, but had heard that it was a nobleman disliked by the Ladies, and they were obliged to put him on the high column fearing the Ladies would punish him by poking his eyes out with their umbrellas'. So much for the City's legend and our Scotchman's sense of humour. Later when saying good bye with our best thanks for his attention, Mr. George pressed his hand very firmly. The writer was the last to leave the table and he became very confidential and in very complimentary tone suggested that we were very fortunate to travel with the Gentleman that had just left the table. I took this at its value and gave him a decided confirmation, but added that we did not need to travel to Edinburgh to learn that.

Our car was garaged about a mile from our Hotel and we suggested that the Ladies get ready whilst we fetched the car. On arriving at the Garage the car was soon made ready, tyres attended to, well oiled and tanks filled with petrol. We than decided for a longer route to the Hotel, which would take us through some of the old streets and lead to Holyrood Palace. At the foot of Arthur Seat the car was turned and we passed places of interest that we had visited the previous day. It reminded us that we were making adieus and our thanks for its courteous kindness to us – visitors from the extreme County of Cornwall, the home of Saints and minerals, with its noble history also of fame and tenacity, for have we not sung "And shall Trelawney die, 20,000 Cornishmen will know the reason why", and thus we think, if Scotland has great History, we oo have pride of Cornwall our own County. We were soon at our Hotel and packing the car with cases that contained travelling requirements. We had the joy of bidding good bye to Miss Harris who had been a good friend, in many ways, during our 64 hours visit.

'HOMEWARD'

We started our homeward track at 11 a.m. Thoughts will often obtrude and question us if we are satisfied with our rest. Human Nature is so demanding in her requirements. One point we consoled ourselves with was that we had put in full time, the 8 hours day had no part or consideration with us. We were on holiday in the glorious months of June/July with their long warm days and nature did not hide the fact. The glow of sunshine brightened every hill and valley and light clouds cast their shadows on the trees and fields, revealing the shades of Gorse and Heather in the valleys and on the distant hills. We were in the North where, of course, we had the advantage of the length in the day. But somehow we could not resist the feeling that with a little more time we could have broadened our excursions.

Cornwall has been sending China Clay from our own Port of Par, to Leith, Boness, Granton, Kirkaldy and Methil, ports on the Firth of Forth; yet we had not even visited Leith, which is only about 2 miles from Edinburgh. In order to compromise this regret we suggested to human nature that if opportunity again presented itself we could then pay our homage and respect to these ports that are receiving our Commerce; thus supplying their need and keeping their Wheels of trade and industry in conditions that spell successful issues to the employee, employer and commerce, thus Cornwall has her link with Scotland.

Our route led us to Carlops and Lockerbie. Here in the town square a very fine memorial was erected to their brave heroes who gave their all in the Great War. We thought it a very beautiful erection and Mr. George, ever on the alert for value, took photographs. We were informed that the cost of erection amounted to nearly £1,000 for a small town we thought the inhabitants were very patriotic. From here we had a view of the Pentland hills.

We were now on very high ground and went on to Biggar and Crawford where we arrived at 12.40 and decided to regale ourselves with refreshment at a wayside Hotel, apparently used by sportsmen. From the road one could see a large tract of gentle sloping fields and rough lands, the atmosphere was very clear giving us a long distance asked, and in the distance we could discern the hills and mountain heights.

The two waitresses at the Hotel gave us fine examples of Midlothian dialect and on listening very carefully we could understand the meaning of some of the phrases. We thought they were blessed with very nimble tongues.

We left this Sportsmen's shelter at 2.5 p.m. Our next stop being at Ecclefechan – Carlyle's birth place – in appearance a cottage home. The camera was again in evidence with two of the party, one at the front door, the other standing by the window. The house has a plate with the announcement that it is the birth place of Thomas Carlyle. What can we say of this learned Scotch moralist, essayist and historian. We learn that he first studied for the ministry, then became a tutor, biographer and farmer. In 1837 he moved from Scotland and his farm home and settled in Cheyne Row, Chelsea. His massive brain gave his pen constant employment. His writings were of noble conception and of incomparable value to the world of literature. His capacity for work was stimulated by the commanding power of mind. The genius of his many literary achievements is demonstrated by a depth of thought so woven in form and matter, that ministers, students and orators must be grateful for the inimitable scope of thought embracing sense and logic with its application to religious, political and social distinctions.

Our next stop was at Gretna Green, and we were now on the border line of Scotland and England. The famous Smithy is situated on the roadside and is also arranged as a museum with the Forge and Fatal Anvil as its central atractions. One of the latest posters announced the recent marriage of the Dutch Giant and shewed his photgraph. This is evidently a place that gives its owners a large source

RYDAL LAKE AND WORDSWORTHS SEAT

LINCHFIELD CATHEDRAL

BOWDEN STONE, BARROWDALE

KENILWORTH CASTLE

of revenue. It also gave a show appearance by the number of wood structures as shops; many cars with casual visitors were also on the roadside.

When we crossed the border on our upward Journey we remember saying "Hail Bonnie Scotland", as we now cross the South border we again salute with our adieus and with a warmth that speaks of a thought that is both kindly and corteous. We shall try and remember your vast treasures of natural scenery, your wealth of refinement so amply displayed in its qualities of goodness and kindness to us strangers who have received pleasure and instruction within your border.

The run from Edinburgh was very enjoyable, we passed over some very high hills and as we descended to the glens, some being beautifully wooded, the colour of the grass suggested fertility. The Glens presented rich woodland pictures, with its perspective of a thin purple haze and colouring of native flowers running through the long valleys to the distant hills.

Boundaries should always claim respect. This is what our feeling was when we left Gretna Green with its Claudestine laws and customs.

We were again on English soil on the Cumberland road, and as our car sped forward we were able to catch a view of Solway Firth. It was refreshing to again see the sea, the restless sea with its mighty power dashing and spreading its foam on the rocks.

We passed through the City of Carlisle at 5.30 p.m., and we remembered Parliamentary controversy during the war, and the question of State purchase versus Licencing reform laws and the establishing of model houses on similar lines to the Swedish plan.

It is from here also that the Roman Wall crosses the Country to Newcastle. It is said that it runs for miles as straight as an arrow and at places the stones are cut with the wheel marks of the Roman Chariots as clear as on the roads of Pompeii.

We are now travelling with expectancy of soon reaching Keswick and the glory of the Lake district. A long length of the road had recently been tar surfacrd and being a bright warm day the heat had made the covering liquified, consequently we had to proceed slowly and cautiously. When about 10 miles from Keswick and on high ground, we noticed something in the distance, apparently as a cone with a low lying cloud. This evidently was the top of one of the Keswick Mountains – Skiddaw or Scaefel.

We were now on a road with a gentle decline for several miles. On our right was a water course, its bed shewing rough boulder rocks giving evidence of conveying the storm torrents during the wet season, although now practically dry. From the edge of this river it stooped down to a wooded valley. On our left a steadily rising embankment, and as our car proceeded we had glimpses, in the embankment spaces, of the hilly lands.

When about 4 miles from Keswick we noticed a wayside Farm House with a notice "Teas Served". We were all needing refreshments and quickly decided to take the advantage of the kindly hospitable notice. We were all delighted with the picturesque place, it presented so much natural rural scenery. The house was at the foot of a mountain high hill, and gave us the impression of a challenge to "Climb me if you can". On the opposite side and in the valley was the Bassenwaite water shewing with the gleam of the late afternoon's sun the stillness and sheen on its surface, with tall trees laden with rich foliage guarding its banks. The question at the tea table, which was laid in a homely way with Cumberland cakes, Short-bread and other appetising enticements which was much enjoyed especially the cup of tea, was shall we stop at this homely resting place to-night or go forward to Keswick. The thought of getting nearer home was with us the limitation of time. It was 7 days since we started and the thought of getting on was gaining influence on our decisions, thus we wisely decided to motor on to Keswick where we arrived at 8.40 p.m. On entering the Town we were met with gaily decorated streets bunting and evergreens. Questions at these triumphal occasions present the thought "Why this ado" our visit was not announced or expected nor were we ambitious for this display of welcome. We considered ourselves fortunate in securing accomodation at a cottage home, the car was garaged. The Lady of the house received us as friends and gave us a welcome that we appreciated. After a rest in which our host freely chatted we enquired why the town was decorated. The answer gave us the sequel to the powerful royal blue car that passed us when we were on the road to Edinburgh, and to which Mr. George called our attention, as previously mentioned. The good Lady was surprised that we had not heard of the Prince's visit.

Her good-will to the Prince gave us a lesson in patriotism and affection – Republicanism had no part or parcel in her nature. Referring to the decoration on her house, this good woman said she had walked 4 miles in order to get this particular foliage. With regret in her

51

voice and in the Cumberland accent said "But the Prince is not looking well, we are hoping he may come to us for a holiday and Keswick will help to restore his vigour.

We were anxious on this Saturday evening to see the Town and visit the Derwent Water which is considered by Keswick people as the Queen of the Lakes. It certainly is a beautiful spot. Motor and other boats are numerous and the boatmen are very anxious for employment. Although it was now getting late, we could not resist the desire for a Cruise. It was a beautiful night, still, calm and peaceful, only the sound of the revolving oar in the water, or the musical sound of the light breeze through the trees with rustling of their foliage which surrounded the lake at its base. From the end we embarked we noticed an Island, the largest in the Lake with a residence built on it, and two others in appearance Fairy Islands, in different parts of the lake. Each were covered with trees like a minature forest. As we were propelled gently along, on the left side we were looking at the steep and rugged clefts and higher up the rounded hill tops with the fading light shewing between their graduated heights. As the boatman turned his craft after reaching the far end, Skiddaw shewed its mountain height, displaying even in the darkening twilight its grimness and defiance and its evening shadows of ruggedness. The boatman and his friend chatted with us very freely and enlarged their conversation with the beauties of the lakes, the various sceneries that could be reached by road and motor and mentioned that one part of the lake reached a depth of 700 feet. It has been said that fossils and shells had been discovered and endurance of the Alpinist to climb its heights.

May we suggest that to the stranger or visitor there is a feeling of awe as one contemplates natures wonders and on looking at this great water basin or lake surrounded by mighty barriers and presided over by majestic mountains. Imagination travels back to the beginning and we ask ourselves 'Who can penitrate natures secrets or who can explain its cause and effect. Dr. Chadwick writing on Creation and contrasting the Bible (Genisis) account with present day thought said science demands millions of years for the age of the Earth. The scientist declares that the rocks record a vast period in the world prior to the beginning of man. The Bible (Genisis) account makes provision for this period for it says, 'The Earth was waste and void and darkness was upon the face of the deep'. The pictorial story may not be scientific in form but it is never unscientific in truth.

Thus in the dateless past Keswick and district bears witness to upheavals, or a lifting of the strata by some internal force or by violent Volcanic eruptions thus recording the forming of the Earth's crust much as we find it now.

As we travelled back to our resting place, the main streets were still alive with people, probably many as ourselves – visitors – we were anxious to hear the music of conversation from folks who had come to their market town to learn the latest business or local news. Our hostess gave us a warm welcome and a light warm supper awaited us. During the meal she gave us interesting lessons on the geography of the lake district, with the result that we decided to make a detour which led us through some of the most beautiful scenery of the district. We were glad to retire for rest, each day had given us thrills of new scenery, probably we may have read of but had not expected to view with their perspective and natural surroundings. Often thoughts of natures goodness and vastness calms and lures one to peaceful sleep.

Our waking thoughts – yes – it is Sunday, and as we looked through the window, we thought what a wonderful country of Ruskin, Southey, Wordsworth, writers and poets of world fame, and what a setting for men of imagination and culture, everywhere you looked nature gave inspiration. The mountains were not all discernable from our window but we knew that we were partaking of Keswicks health giving cordials. Its atmosphere was wafted through our open window and consisted of so many elements. We knew we were breathing a moisture that consisted of the breeze from the mountains, the perfumes of the trees and flowers, the moisture from the lakes and the haze and fog from the valley. We knew also that if Keswick district distilled this elixir it could not be returned to the area, but prepared and wafted by every wind for the healing of the nations. The invisable things and influences that God has prepared are greater that the visible, "eye has not seen, neither the ear heard............

Our conversation at the breakfast table – Could we have the day by the lake side? We again had to think in terms of duty. It was necessary for us to be home on the following Thursday and this could not be effected if we followed our desire. Consequently we decided to push forward. At 10.30 we said thanks to our kindly hostess, who gave us with parting words a pressing invitation to come back to Keswick for a good holiday and at her home.

We followed this Ladies suggested route which led us again through the main street by the Town Hall in the Tower of which hangs a bell bearing the date of 1001, which is said to have come from the ancestral seat of the Earl of Derwentwater. As we passed an elevated position or crag on the bank of the lake when returning from our cruise the previous evening, our friends directed our attention to Ruskin's monument erected in 1900 and bearing on the one side a bronze medallion with the following inscription:-

"The first thing I remember as an event in life
"was being taken by my nurse to the brow of Trears
"Crag, Derwantwater."

on the reverse side is another inscription viz:-

"The Spirit of God is around you in the air that
"you breathe His glory in the light that you see
"and in the fruitfulness of the earth and the
"joy of its creatures. He has written for you
"day by day His revelation as He has granted you
"day by day your daily bread"

When we think of how beautiful the opening of the Child mind is, cannot it be likened to the gradual opening of the flower. Tracing the gracious and wonderful gifts to the Child from the Divine as the petal of the flower opening to bloom to perfection. We notice as first, memory's record, and as this block of stone erected in the position of keeping vigil over the peaceful waters indicating the spot with its indelible effect on the child. Not doubt this occasion had its influence on the after ideals that was so entwined in his life and letters. As we think of the Barrowdale Stone standing with its reflective message and as a silent yet effective preacher with its inspiring message that the Spirit of God is around you... His glory is in the light &c.&c.&c. Thus on the Crag with its tall trees shading it and mossy grass as its carpet looking over the beauty of the lake and wildness of the mountains stretching to the Heavens, and with the passing clouds portraying their ever changing colours. We could not leave Keswick and the Derwentwater without referring to this monument which reveals so much of reverend thought to Ruskin.

We also thought of the Annual Convention of world wide interest that is held at Keswick, and which is attended by Ministers, and Laymen without reference to name or denomination, drawings its large attendance of 6000 people, with its appeal to College and University Students and those who are anxious to work for Christ and the deepening of the life of God in the heart. From this Convention many Students of both seas and others embrace the service for God with its sublimity or purpose to World Wide evangilisation.

As we started our Journey on this Sunday morning we had no idea that pleasures on the Sabbath day had become so popular.

The road from Keswick to Grasmere led us over some high hills giving us a very interesting landscape view of this part of the Lake district. In passing over Dunmail Raise, with its extensive view, we met several charabancs laden with pleasure seekers evidently from Morcombe Bay and district, suggesting that the lure of the open and Sunday pleasure excursions was very manifest.

We could not pass Grasmere without visiting Wordsworth's early home. This proved to be a well built cottage which has been acquired by the nation as a Wordsworth Museum. We entered the garden and looked through the windows. At the side entrance a verandah protected the door with a corner seat. We could not resist the impulse of sitting in his seat, and we wondered if this was the seat and place where inspiring thought came to the poet whom Andrew Long describes as "the poetic secret of nature was waiting for Wordsworth" Listen to his Poem on early recollections or intimations of immortality from recollections of early childhood:—

> "There was a time when meadow, grove and stream,
> "The earth and every common sight
> "to me did seem
> "Apparelled in Celestial light.
>
> ...   .
>
> "The rainbow comes and goes,
> "look around her when the Heavens are bare.
> "Waters on a starry night
> "are beautiful and fair

This poem concludes:—

"I love the Brooks which down their Channels fret,
"Even more than when I tripped lightly as they:
"The innocent brightness of a new born day
"Is lovely yet.
"The clouds that gather round the setting run
"Do take a sober colouring from an eye
"That has kept watch o'er man's morality.
"Another race has been, and other palms are won
"Thanks to the human heart by which we live.
"Thanks to its tenderness, its joys and fears,
"To me the meanest flower that blows can give
"Thoughts that do often be too deep for tears.

...　　...　　...　　...　　...　　...　　...　　...

The drive from Grasmere, Rydal and Ambleside to Windermere was very charming, with the lake scenery on one side and on the other overhanging trees, which at places appeared as archways and looked as if they were suspended from the cliff and hillside heights. We could also feel the cooling breeze from the lake.

We learn that the Windermere is 10 miles long and 1 mile wide. To the seeker after rest there is so much in this district to interest and it offers pastime and pleasure in various ways and forms. To the fisherman, sportsman, Alpinist, botanist, naturalist and scientist in general, the lake district abounds even to natural extremes with undescriptive wealth i the formation of its majestic hills and lovely valleys, its high mountains and deep ravines and passes, its lakes with their ever varying cloud and sky shades. At Bowness one would think we were arriving at a shipping port with its wide and long pier for the use of boatmen and visitors. A large number of boats of various lengths and sizes some motor or steam, sailing and paddling boats and canoes were moored in ship-shape style each side of the Pier. They were all beautifully fitted with cabin and cushion, everything for comfort and pleasure. Swans instead of Gulls were numerous and gave quite a gala appearance. The camera was again used for this pretty scene, and also as a copy of the principal shipping port of this inland sea, – Windermere Lake.

We stopped here for 20 minutes. This is indeed a popular and busy port with the rush of car and bus and the preparation being made by the boatmen for the afternoon, and the visitors standing or seated on the pier, and promenade seats. Somehow this did not appeal to us, no doubt it was the day that had its influence. Thinking of the road we had just come along we should have liked time and opportunity, before bidding adieu to the lake country, to have visited with leisure some of its famous places and scenic beauty spots, that we could walk along the road that we had just run over, that we could rest and read by the lakes, whose water at places came near to the road surface. We also remembered we had been travelling near the home of Southey, Wordsworth and Ruskin and other writers whom history delights to honour.

On leaving Bowness we had to climb one of the hilly roads that form the basin of the lake district. Although it was very steep the car faced its duty without hesitation. On reaching the summit the wind was fresh, keen and refreshing and on each side of the road and for a long distance we had an excellent view of the formation and the rugged hill-tops. We were now travelling in the County of Westmorland.

After a run of 10 miles we arrived at Kendall at 1.45 with the feeling that we were all ready for lunch. Our necessity was bountifully met at the principal hotel, which was, we presumed, a very ancient house and provided with extensive courtyard and stabling at the rear. If this house could relate its history it no doubt would speak of having accomodated many noble Knights and Chavalliers when on the business of King and Country.

We started again at 2.50 with the hope of reaching Buxton as our resting place for the night.

We passed through Kirby, Lonsdale and Giggleswick. Naturally we were much interested here as this was one of the eclipse centres and which the papers reported gave one of the best views of the eclipse. From this aspect if we had taken the West instead of the East totallity line we should, no doubt, have had a greater reward, but this does not imply that we were not gratified with the priviledge we had at Richmond. Memory will always connect us with the eclipse's wonderful vision and effect of what we witnessed. We still think of the observation, the shadow, the chilliness and shades with the effect it had on the concourse of the people, cattle and farm yard stock.

The road was very interesting from Giggleswick to Skipton and furnished us with ideas of Sunday pleasure. The wide road was bounded on the left with a red rock cleft and on the other side trees were planted at regular spaces up the steep embankment. It gave us a

THE LIZARD LIGHTS

POLKERRIS HARBOUR

SHAKESPEAR'S BIRTHPLACE, STRATFORD-ON-AVON

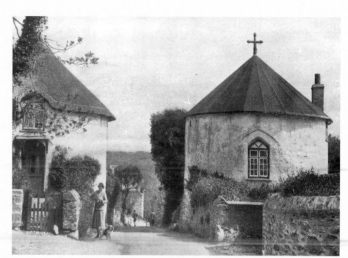

ROUND HOUSES OF ST. VERYAN

KYNANCE COVE, THE LIZARD.

220971.

pleasant outlook over a long range of green fields. As we were travelling we could feel the cool Southerly breeze with its cooling effect and exhilaration to the mind.

We were soon cognisant that we had entered a holiday sphere. Every space between the trees was occupied by a family and a car, table cloths and pic-nic arrangement laid on the grass. The laughter and evident delight of the children and families gave us a vision of the seeker after the open life and also thought of what the future was going to be like. Coming into the town of Skipton we had quite a mass of cars to negotiate. The street was broad and the parking ground was arranged in the centre and the number of cars was legion and quite gave us the impression of a gala or public holiday. We noticed the garages had a very active time in supplying petrol and attending to minor repairs. At one point the pressure of cars was so continuous that we were obliged to wait opportunity to proceed.

Our next stop was at Halifax where we arrived at 5.40. We were now anxious for a cup of tea and a passing gentleman directed us to a hotel. We presumed is the THE hotel of Halifax by its splendour of apartment and the livery of its waiters. We were accomodated in the lounge and tea was served in a charming manner. This was indeed a dainty and posh affair. After tea, a rest and home writing and a walk to the General Post Office. We passed on the way a Salvation Army band who were commencing a service in an open space. We could only stop for a few minutes and the band gave us a very homely rendering of one of their popular hymns, and it gave us cheer and thought. Halifax we thought was a busy town, and the hotel gave us a unique tea and rest at a cost of 1/– each. We were again ready for the road at 6.40 and a run of about 8 miles brought us to the town of Huddersfield, the town of football fame. We passed through the level of this industrial town and noticed the Derbyshire heights luming above the houses, and as we got nearer a narrow road became visible looking like a piece of sig-siz brown ribbon. We had to climb this mountain hill of 1750 feet (Woodhead by name). On reaching the top the contrast was very apparent; at the top hats had to be secured because the wind was very strong. It was also very interesting to look over the way we had just travelled. The town appeared very flat, on the side of the hill we noticed reservoirs apparently for the water supply of the town. The short stop on the mountain pass was very exhilarating and we should have enjoyed a long halt there but we remembered that we had several miles to travel yet and the pass on the other side to negotiate. As our car descended we noticed we were on the edge of a deep ravine. It appeared in places, as if the road had been cut through the solid

Derbyshire stone. At places we wondered at the skill of the wall builders, the land divisions were hedged with solid stone from the valley to the precipitious and extreme edge of the highest peak. We admired the stability and the ingenious and dangerous work of the builder which we thought was one of the wonders of the pass.

We came through Woodhead and arrived at Glossop at 9 p.m. I think we all needed rest and decided to seek accomodation for the night instead of pressing on to Buxton. We were very comfortably entertained at one of the leading hotels which was near Glossop station.

On entering the town we passed crowds of young women who had probably been for long walks on the Derbyshire hills, all without exception attired so as to present taste and even culture in apparel; shade and style apparently was actual thought to them.

After a light and satisfying meal, a pleasant chat and review of the day, for we had travelled Cumberland, Westmorland, the edge of Lancashire, Yorkshire and were now resting in Derbyshire. We thought this should reward us with a good nights rest and with this thought retired.

Very early in the morning our party were awakened by a sound of a multitude of dogs on the pavement. Many of the girls who had presented the fairy-like appearance of the previous evening were off to the station and to their employment as mill workers at Manchester and the various Mills of the district.

We left Glossop at 10 o'clock for Buxton. We were now travelling at a height of 1000 feet above sea level. We passed natural lime burrows similar in appearance to our Clay burrows. The town lies in a hollow and we all thought we could not pass through this famous Hydro without satisfying our enquiring minds, especially as this was the celebrated Derbyshire health restoring resort. We noticed several people with stick or crutch indicating pain or sorrow and suffering. I think our thought as we returned to the car was that the many people who visit this famous Hydro and seek its Baths and raryfied air may rejoice in restoration and healing vigour.

As we left the town the car was stopped for Petrol, and we always had the feeling that it had taken us over many long roads and had not once refused any duty it was pressed to do, so it deserved full measure of lubricant and petrol. We happened to stop near a Wesleyan church and noticed the following printed or painted on a large board at the entrance:

"To all who are struggling and need strength,

"Weary and need courage,

"Alone and need friendship

"This church offers a welcome".

With the sick and crippled from home and friends we thought this notice should be of great comfort to the visitor who need strength, courage and friendship and we hoped both Minister and congregation are reverend and attentive to these Ministrations.

We left Buxton at 11.40 to continue our journey homeward. On passing Sudbury and district the farms appeared to be well cultivated and the crops in fine condition. We enjoyed the drive of 47 miles to Lichfield (Staffordshire) the county of Pottery renown.

Our first necessity was Lunch which was soon arranged, and after which we had a walk through the main street and then to the Cathedral. We admired the beautifully ornamented West front and we thought the main entrance doorway was very low and small in comparison to the stately front. The sacred edifice was built of red or dark ochre shade stone and to us looked very heavy in appearance, but apparently by its mouldings and carvings it has withstood the test of time and atmosphere. The interior gives one an idea of the architects perfect imagination and the builders and sculptors understanding and ability. Workmen of these days surprise us with the unique character, the magnificence and durability of their work, truly they worked for the future. We admired the stone carvings, the pillars tall and massive, its ceilings and beautifully coloured glass windows, the glass of which is said to be equal to any in the United Kingdom, and it is of Flemish manufacture. The total length of the Cathedral is 371 ft. The first Cathedral was built by St. Chad 700 A.D., and the present one was commenced 1135 on the foundation of the former. It was restored in the year 1908 at a total cost of £98,000 and the aim then was to bring the cathedral back to the Harmony and beauty of its original scheme.

Lichfield has the honour of being the birth place of Dr. Samuel Johnston (1709) the lexicographer and writer who it was said was the most prominent literary man in England. His famous dictionary was published in 1755. He was also a voloumous writer and it is said was greatly honoured during his life and accorded burial in Westminster Abbey. His biography was written by James Boswell and thought to be one of the best written in the English language.

We left here at 3.40 for Kenilworth Castle (Warwickshire) a distance of about 34 miles. It was a pleasant afternoon for motoring as the sunshine and clouds gave the country a pleasant appearance with its alternate brightness and shade, the effect of passing clouds. We arrived at the entrance gate at 5 p.m. and were admitted to the Castle Ruins after paying the usual fee. As we approached the derilect pile of building one could not but be impressed with the thought of vandalism and what of the past. There is something about the place that seems to create a saddening effect. As one walked over the walls of vast thickness every portion massive, this castle with dimensions built for the centuries but now just and enclosure of departed glory we think it would be well to give an extract from the Encyclopaedia Britannica bearing on its History:—

"......The manor of Kenilworth was bestowed by Henry I
"(1100-1135) on Geoffrey de Clinton afterwards Lord
"Chief Justice who erected the earlier part of the
"Castle. By his grandson Henry de Clinton it was
"given to King John and it remained in the Royal
"family until the time of Henry III (1216-1272) who
"granted it to Simon de Montfort, Earl of Leicester.
"After the battle of Evesham 14 August 1265 at which
"Simon de Montfort was slain the rebel forces rallied
"at the Castle when it sustained a siege for six
"months, but finally capitulated to Henry III who
"bestowed it on his son Edmund. After being used as
"a prison of Edward II previous to his removal to
"Berkeley it came into the possession of John of Gaunt
"by whom it was greatly enlarged. On his son becoming
"King as Henry IV (1399-14130 it was made a Royal
"Residence and it remained the possession of the Crown
"until Queen Elizabeth who in 1562 granted it to Robert
"Dudley, Earl of Leicester who spent a large sum in
"restoring it and whose splendid entertainments there
"to Queen Elizabeth are described in Scotts Novel
"° 'Kenilworth'. During the Civil War it was dismantled
"by the soldiers of Cromwell and it was thenceforth
"abandoned to decay. Since the restoration 1660 it
"has belonged to the House of Clarendon. The walls of
"the Castle originally enclosed an area of 7 acres the
"principal portion of the building still remaining are
"the Gatehouse, now used as a dwellinghouse, Carsar's
"Tower, the only portion built by Goffrey de Clinton
"now extant, with massive walls sixteen feet thick,
"Gaunt with windows of very beautiful design and the
"Leicester buildings which are in a very ruinous
"condition"

The Castle was built of a dark red sand stone which is very durable. We bade adieu to the Ruins and Castle Grounds at 5.30. Visitors were still arriving on the same errand and motors were lined up at the entrance gateway. These ancient places and their History appeals to a large international public proving the statements of the American Lady that we read your History and fiction and are anxious to view their settings hence our visit to England.

Let us quote here from Sir Walter Scotts Historic Novel 'Kenilworth' depicting the affluence and gaiety of the castle in the Reign of Queen Elizabeth.

"......As the Queen left the threshold of her chamber,
"Leicester was by her side and proposed to her a walk
"in the gardens, to this scene of pleasure they
"walked. The Earls arm affording the Sovereign the
"occasional support which she required when climbing
"flights of steps, then a favourite ornament in a
"garden, conducting them from terrace to terrace.
"The ladies in attendance gifted with prudence did
"not conceive it their duty to follow the Queen's person
"closely or to approach so near to share or disturb the
"conversations between the Queen and the Earl. They
"contented themselves by admiring the grace of this
"illustrious couple. Elizabeth's sylvan dress which
"was of pale blue silk with silver lace &c well suited
"to her height and the dignity of her mien, Leicester
"his hunting suit of Lincold Green richly embroidered
"with Gold and crossed by gay baldire.............
"The Earl had in his vanity and ambition on in both
"thrown more of that delicious ingredient until he
"unfortunately became the language of love itself.
" 'No Dudley' said Elizabeth, yet it was with broken accent,
" 'No, I must be the mother of my people, other ties that
"makes the lowly maiden happy are denied to her sovereign
" – No Leicester, urge it no more – were I as others,
"free to seek my own happiness, then indeed – but it
"cannot, cannot be, now leave me My Lord' ". 'How I leave
"you Madam, has my madness offended you.' No Leicester
"not so', answered the Queen hastily. While she spoke
"thus Dudley bowed deeply and retired with a slow and
"melancholy air. The Queen stood gazing after him and
"murmered to herself – 'Were it possible – were it but
"possible – but no – no Elizabeth must be the wife and
"mother of England alone'. Ere she proceeded she had
"recovered her dignity of look, and her mien its air of
"command"

We are now on or way to Stratford on Avon a distance of about 14 miles, and en route we were soon passing the famous Warwick Castle. This is one of the most interesting Castles in the Country, and stands on an elevation overlooking the river Avon. This was once the home of the famous Earl of Warwick known to History as the King maker, who was leader of the York party in the Wars of the Roses, and carried his ambitious plans with great energy and success. He was killed at War in the Battle of Barnet.

The Countess of Warwick is identified with many popular movements for the betterment of her sex, was an ardent advocate on the platform and in the press, has established colleges, hostels and scientific and technical schools and a home at Warwick for crippled children. Is this not a contrast between War and Power, and education and the love of the things that master, prompted by sympathy and the desire for service to make a better England "A land for heroes to live in."

We knew we were travelling on Historic ground, and were nearing the famous town of Stratford on Avon, the Birth place of William Shakespeare (1564-1616) Englands greatest Poet and Dramatist. He was the eldest son of a tradesman and married Ann Hathaway who was 8 years his senior, five years after his marriage he went to London. He first came to prominence as a Poet in 1593 and then as Actor and Playwright at the Globe and other Theatres which no doubt led to his remarkable career. His plays became, and are now, the wonder of the world. About 1612 he returned from London to his native home where he died at the age of 52 and was buried in Stratford Church. His genius is worshipped by every nation. All nations are anxious to take their part in the manifestation and honour and gratitude to this great man who knew human nature and was able in a high degree to express it in his plays and sonnets. The greatness of his work after close on 350 years has the same remarkable attraction and in all Countries and Languages this visit to Stratford on Avon was one of the Crowning events of our holiday.

Entering the town by crossing the peaceful water and looking toward the church with its tall steeple, where lies the remains of the Worlds hero, and then through the thronged streets to the Parking ground. The centre of this wide main street is used for this purpose and parked a long line of cars of all makes and descriptions on each side of the parking ground and the whole length of the street.

The National flags of all Nations were displayed on tall flagstaffs, it being Gala week. We were informed that Germany had again this year re-established her claim to honour the Illustrious and beloved Shakespeare by rehoisting the German National Flag.

How can we express the thrill of a walk through this principle street made gay with the floating of the flags of the World. No other Poet or man of distinction has been honoured, and each year on this anniversary day, as what we can safely say super International man. We visited his Birth place with its oak panneled front, as we have previously seen in many books and pictures. The whole street has evidently fixed in this picturesque style, even the hotels who served us with refreshment has its decorations with oak tables and seats to match. We regret time would not permit us to visit Ann Hathaway's Cottage, we presumed it would now shew its floral beauty.

The town appeared to be invaded with people of all Nationalities. We thought the Americans were in the majority, de-lux and stately cars and busses gave us an animated time when leaving the town there being so many wearing horn rim spectacles and the difference in the attire, suggested friends from across the Atlantic. Before leaving we visited Shakespeares memorial Theatre which was still roof less caused by the fire.

Canon Deane in his Lecture on Shakespeare said "The "motive that brought Shakespeare back to his own place was "his soul and the lessons that each one of us in this "feavered life whould seek opportunity for discerning the "Invisible and being attuned to the Eternal"

Fortune favours the seeker in the fact that our visit to Stratford on Avon was on remembrance day or Gala week. We should have enjoyed leisure here as there were so many Historic places we should have enjoyed visiting, but we all became obsessed with the get along home feeling and even here could not suppress the thought of getting forward to Cheltenham our next stopping and resting place, a distance of about 30 miles.

The roads were very fine here for motoring and led us through Broadway (Warwickwhire) which is a very large Fruit growing district. It was interesting to trace the long rows of trees with wide spaces between intended for soft fruits or vegetables. We noticed the orchards had a gentle slope southward which gave protection from the North winds and the advantage of the morning sun. The trees were all of

WATERFALLS, LUXYLIAN, PAR

ST. MARTINS IN THE FIELDS

PAR, BEACH HUTS

medium size and the bark looked very clean. With our interest in fruit growing we should have enjoyed the priviledge of a walk in the orchards, thus giving us an opportunity for closer observation.

We arrived at Cheltenham at 9.30 pm. Our first impression as we descended the hill leading to the town – Yes, this is a beautiful place. The wide street with residential houses on each side, wide pavements either side,and we noticed that these indicated rain the people were hastening with open umbrellas. We soon came to the tram lines which led us to our hotel. We had good accomodation and attention given to our comfort. At the supper table we again tried to visualise the long distance we had travelled and the historic places we had visited. We were all ready now for Natures restorer rest and sleep.

We met at the Breakfast table at 9 a.m. and were reminded it was Tuesday. These morning chats gave us an ideal opportunity of arranging our time table and often a good laugh or cheering joke. After breakfast we had a walk through some of the principle streets. Shop windows contained some very expensive dressings and this was not without interest to us. We noticed the town was also an horticultural centre. At open spaces the electric light standards were fitted at the base with a circular reservoir which was very beautifully and tastefully laden with flowers and greenery. This was the first town where we had seen this example of flora decoration during our travel, except, of course, in the public parks.

We returned to our Hotel and were soon ready to continue our journey. Before leaving the town we motored to the colleges, and had an interesting time watching the large number of pupils and professors, who were robed, entering the college from the robing rooms. The students gave us the idea of smartness and were there for physical and mental training. We again motored through the town with the hope of reaching Bath (Somerset) in time for Lunch, a distance of about 35 miles.

On our way to Bath was passed the village of Painswick, celebrated for its cemetry containing 99 yew trees. Legend says that if a hundred were planted one always dies. We arrived at Bath at 1.30 p.m.

It has been said that nature was in her bountiful mood when Bath was moulded, with the river Avon in its winding course wandering across the city displaying its cooling water and the verdure of its banks and its bridges as an added interest. Bath has earned the name of

Queen of the West. The guide to Bath advises the visitor to pay a visit to Buchen Cliff, which affords delight and pleasure to the visitor being 400 ft above the Avon. Our road into Bath led us down from a lofty aminence giving us a superb view of the City with its churches and steeples, its public buildings recognised by their spaciousness and then the winding of the streets and river, and the famous houses and homes of poets, men of letters, Politicians, Scientists and others of fame, whose record and history has been indelibly recorded in the pages of history.

The Bath stone has given the City building a characteristic and greyness all its own, and has been adapted for practically every building purpose and lends itself to architecture of the most refined and life-like expression.

We garaged the car and repaired to one of the popular restaurants for Lunch, after ordering from the menu card we enjoyed the pleasure of being again satisfied, and decided to limit our time to one hour and each to meet the car at the agreed time. Mr. & Mrs. George arranged to visit the Abbey, which is said to be the latest of the great perpendicular Gothic works in the country. The edifice was completed in the reign of Queen Elisabeth. There is a marvellous harmony with its wonderful pillars and traced roof and the west entrance with its magnificent carved door, a building of charm. Mrs. Parkyn and myself visited the Roman Baths, a very wonderful place indeed. It is said the City has more Roman remains than any other place in the United Kingdom. One needs time to rush through the apartments, spaces and corridors, so much unearthed monuments and broken remains being stored by the walls. A notice stated that 'This great Roman bath was finally laid open in 1883'. The enclosure of the bath is 111'4" from East to West by 68'6" wide. There are recessed on either side with seats and alcoves presumed used for disrobing. The platform around the Bath is about 14 feet wide and steps of massive masonry lead down to the bath. Apparently by the large stone piers still standing, the bath was covered in its early history and from the manner in which the pavements have been identified and with its worn appearance it is very evident that this large bath was much frequented by the Ancients over a long period, probably many centuries.

The museum contains a large number of coins, pottery &c. When one looks at this wonderful building with its healing water, massive pillars and traceries, its balcony and the extremely fine carvings, which was built about 2000 years ago and still remains to challenge the centuries one has to think in terms of Genius of a very clever and industrious race of men who worked for the future.

The grand Pump room gives one an idea of spacious restfulness used by water drinkers and bathers. In this room is a very fine fountain of marble with steaming water coming from the mysterious depths of the earth. It is said the water has an agreable taste and is reviving to the spirits. This room leads to the baths of many systems, and one is amazed at this wonderful phenomona of nature. This hot steaming water building up from time immemorial containing ingredients of minerals and radium for the alleviation of pain and the healing of the nations. The prehistoric history of Bath contains so much imagination and takes us back to the Bladud legend of the swine and the mud.

The Roman occupation in a.d. 49 is everywhere evident by its baths, walls, buildings, coins and pottery. It is stated that Hadrian a.d. 100 founded a college of armourers.

We did not waste our time but we could not refrain from giving a limited portion to the floral decorations of the shops. It was the season of carnations, and their size, perfume and colouring gave us much pleasure.

We were each at the car at the time appointed and it was now 3.30 p.m. We left by the Bristol road through Corston and Marksbury and Ferrington Gourney for Wells a distance of about 21 miles, where we arrived at 4.15 p.m.

Wells is a place of great antiquity, and history states that the present see was founded in the year 909. Among the well known Bishops of Wells are the names of Wolsey, Fox, Laud and others. The Cathedral is considered to be the most beautiful of English Ecclesiastical edifices. Its famous West front with its 600 matchless sculptured figures, 151 of which are life size, being of remarkable beauty and grandeur. The central tower is 160 feet high and the two western towers 130 high. The interior of the Cathedral is very beautiful and, it is said, where sunshine is natural. The arches seem to fill their arranged positions with wonderful skill, the pillars are wonderfully wrought and carved. The Vicars close is like the gate that gives access to it. It is a little street or cloister flanked on each side by cottages, with roofs and chimneys of great age and beauty. The Bishops palace is a building magnificent and beautiful set on a moat as on a fairy island with its drawbridge and strong walls. We walked through the cloisters and waited to hear the celebrated clock strike which is arranged by men coming from a recess hidden from view until the time for striking, the bell is then struck with hammers according to the hour. Apparently the clock was made with its unique arrangement by monks 400 years ago. In the cathedral grounds the stillness and resplendent sheen on the water of the moat on this summer afternoon, made us anxious to linger and enjoy the chaderal beauty. It has been said 'Many are the buildings that impress, few are those which raise the finer feelings. Time forbade us to halt longer and we were soon on our way to Glastonbury Abbey.

As far as the town is concerned we did not regard it as an attractive place. There are two fine examples of 15th century architecture – The Georges inn and the Tribunal used in olden days as a pilgrims rest. It was not the town we had come to explore. Our thoughts were occupied with this as the landing place of Joseph of Arimathesa and his helpers. It is siad no spot can hold more wonders, store of legend and pure romance or where runs the golden thread of truth. This being the first spot in all our homeland to hear the tidings, Glastonbury was then an island and its Tor about 500 feet above sea level, was, no doubt, the guide to the missionary and his helpers.

Let us attempt to picture these grey ruins of the Abbey set in peaceful green grass and surrounded with trees. Roofless, a standing wreck and yet giving a fine and subdueing appearance with its sculptured walls and massive and other window openings, a turret and beautifully designed short pinacle or tower, all witnessing in its desolation to a great and glorious past.

We noticed that excavations were still in progress, and watching them at their task we could see the careful handling of tools.

Notices or labels were placed at certain parts of the interior. At one place – "St. Dunstans Chapel" another read "The Lady Chapel erected on the site of the original Church 1184", another, "Probable site of the Altar of Joseph of Arimathaea", the pavement still intact. As we returned we could not restrain the deep feeling, this is Avolon the centre of chivalry that knights even gave their life for. As we stepped from the gateway and on looking to our right we could see Glastonbury Tor where at its foot it is said Saint Joseph buried the Holy Grail, the quest of King Arthur and his Knights, and as St. Joseph leant on his staff in prayer, a thorn tree came on the spot, and every year at Christmastide it bursts into blossom, severe weather does not prevent it flowering, and below was the blood stream and its source the Holy Grail. Here too is the burial place of St. Patrick, King Edgar and of the noble Arthur and his Queen Guinevere.

We left this place of deep interest and tradition at 6.30 p.m. for Exeter a distance of about 54 miles.

We again passed through Street and the Historic Athelney so allied to King Arthur as his hiding place, who here so humanly burnt the cakes. We were now on the Taunton road. Let us say here Zummerset is a fine old county, its records are full of tradition and exploits, its villages so picturesque with thatched and quaint shaped roofed houses, presenting their peaceful and homelike appearance. Viewing the county from the Mendips it gives the impression of a level flat marshland to the distant town of Taunton, and as one gets nearer one finds the land intersected by drainage furrows which lead to the more central and larger leats or rivers. These boundary leats or rivers giving growth to the withey on their banks which provides material for the Basket maker and Fisherman.

Looking over this vast field with towns, villages and Churches with their steeples shewing between the tall trees, one can easily imagine that in the distant past this was claimed by the Atlantic and one can almost picture its surf and waves playing on the coast line of the Mendips.

The Mendips are honeycombed with caverns those at Cheddar are considered wonderful and well worth a visit from any part of England, the forms, shapes and colourings of the stalactites and stalagmites are beyond description. Other caves have been partially explored, prehistoric remains of human and wild animals have been discovered, shewing that these caves had been used as dwelling by prehistoric cavemen.

A passing thought here also desired us to refresh our memories with a holiday at Crooks Peak, there is so much abouth this district we should like to recall. This is one of the highest points of the Mendips, our 'digs', the farmhouse, at the bottom. Climbing to the top was not an easy task, the rock held little soil and the short grass was tough and slippery. The ascent was worth the trouble and rewarded us with a wondorous view of the plains of Sommerset. Away on the right, Weston-super-mare, the river Severn and in the distance the Welsh hills. Then turning to the left we followed the course of the Mendips, with the distant view of Taunton to the left. Walking on the summit of these rocks, quite bare at places, and to the opposite side one faces the steep decline to the valley with its sheltered fields growing the greenest of pasture, furnishing the key to the champion Cheddar Cheese.

The sunset from the peak gives a wonderful effect, the golden spears and sprays of light appear to be reflected on this, natures stronghold, and ones memory becomes charged with the splendour of the going down of the sun. The ear is also appealed to by the musical tolling of the Church bells calling the faithful to prayer. There are so many spires one can locate. With the rarefield air the tingle of the bells appears to convey its music vibrating natures and moves the heart to the act of worship. As the light fades the air becomes moist and shades of evening have dulled the brightness of flower and landscape. One leaves the peak filled with thoughts of pleasure and gratitude. A walk from this peak on the Bristol road to Cheddar village and to Burrington Coombe, where, at this famous village Toplady wrote his famous hymn "Rock of Ages". This hymn has been a stronghold to Christian Faith and experience and was written during a thunder storm and the writer sheltered between these mighty rocks.

The traveller finds interest at every point and turn of the road. The farm houses are commodious and attractive in architectural appearance with spacious cattle yards and quite an array of out-buildings. One has to remember that they are practically pasturage farms and the buildings fitted with cheese and cider making appliances. It is a unique pleasure to chat with the Farm worker, one learns the great interest he has in the farm stock and apple growing orchards but not least the entertainment of his happy contented manner and sommerset dialect.

The strawberry gardens near Cheddar are renowned for the quality and rich juices of its fruit and as one reaches Cheddar village with its cheese market, its stream of water from the rocks, its caves and the wonderful gorge with its towering solid limestone rocks reaching to dizzy heights. But we must not forget that to Sommerset and Avalon, England owes a great debt. This land of tradition has helped to mould the character and destiny of our National, for it was at Avalon that St. Joseph of Aramathaea founded the first Christian church. With this digression and obtruding thought we returned to the car and the road. We had an evening view of the Marconi transmission station at Somerton near Bridgewater, with its high pylons and their attachments. We do not think of these stations as local but rather as an international messenger with its mechanical appliances tuned to the invisible world of ether, invading and compassing the Continents of the world with natural voice and sound.

We passed through Illchester, Illminster & Honiton, thus evading Taunton the gate of Sommerset from the West, with its castle and chequered history, bearing the pride of County town and with her network of branch railway lines.

We are now on the roads of glorious Devon passing through pretty perfumed roads protected with flowering hedges, avenues of green and wild flowers and reached Exeter and our hotel at 9.45 p.m.

After a refreshing wash and brush up we enjoyed a light meal which was quickly laid for us. Our conversation after a day travel was usually retrospective recounting the episodes of the day and this suggested many questions for discussion. We had had a full day and in order to reach Exeter, time would not permit us to stop for tea.

We met at the breakfast table at 9 a.m. and our thoughts were based on the question of this being the day to terminate our holiday. This would be the 12th day on the road and I suppose we each had the lurking feeling that we had not the courage to express, that the pleasure of going away from home was equal in compensation with the joy of getting back again. We were unanimous in the thought that changes are necessary and we had enjoyed the unique opportunity of travelling through several of our English counties and Scotland, and gained an education of thought, to think of things we had seen giving us a new grip on life, shewing us the long friendly road, and hope it has helped us to get a new hold on God.

We decided to give a little time in exploring the City. This is not our first visit to Exeter. We enjoyed walking through the narrow main street, where the motor traffic, even in the mornings, is practically congested. The business houses have a personality all their own, each house differing in architecture and probably all pre 1800 types. We visited the 12th century Cathedral, a noble edifice, and we thought the picturesque west front was shewing signs of age or decay. When one considers the many centuries it has weathered the elements withstanding in its glory, sun, rain, wind, frost and snow, one is surprised at its stability. As we entered its sacred precincts, matins were being said and we sat for a portion of the service, and its influence was a direction to our thoughts. We were also anxious to

PAR BEACH AND CLIFFS

THE AQUEDUCT, LUXYLIAN, PAR.

CRINNIS BEACH, PAR

FAMOUS CORNISH OUTCROP. Roche Rock.

inspect a Roman pavement at the Court house. In this we were disappointed as a magistrates meeting was in progress, and the officer in charge gave us a cordial invitation to return later but we were now anxious to get forward.

We were soon in the car and leaving the City and we passed over the beautiful river Exe. This river must be a source of great pleasure especially for boating, swimming and aquatic sports. We passed through Newton Abbot at 12.20 pm.m and we recognised this as a Great Western Railway depot with its extensive engineering and wagon works, its enlarged station and its river Teign used for conveying ball clay by barges to Teignmouth for shipment. We were now on the new or widened road leading to Torquay, the "Queen of the South". The busy streets gave us the impression of a commercial or business town on coming into view of Torbay. I think we all shared the desire of a long stop or an extended holiday here. Torbay was looking at its best with the sunshine playing on its crested water, the Yachts and boats studding the surface and dipping or rolling to the wave and sea breeze, the harbour with its breakwater added to the marine importance.

The promenade, pavillion and winter gardens all gave enchantment and impresses the visitor with the Town's concern for their pleasure. We were now on the Paignton road and looking back with our parting glance to this "Queen of the West", here we see the vision and imagination of Torquay Council and their love for the beautiful. Her natural hills have with the aid of landscape and rock gardeners or architects become gardens of beauty, of rest and peace to the leisured; with its arbours and alcoves, its terraced walks and comfortable seats, the bramble has given place to the fir and lovely flowers and blossoms and from these warm rocks of eminence Torbay with its sceanic beauty stretches away to its background of cliffs and rocks. The searcher for health and quiet has here the ideal spot, overlooking the constant movement of sea and road, inhaling the refreshing ozone prepared by the warmth of the sun and the invigorating perfume of tree, shrub and flower.

The difficulty of travelling by car with its necessary speed, and our enclosure, gives at the best only a passing glance. We found that ones faculties of eye and ear has to be changed with a sense of alertness or the opportunity of even seeing the distant hills or view of the interest of the roadside was quickly passed. Mr. George knew parts of the country so well that the car was not allowed to pass places of Historic interest without our attention being appealed to.

Our next stop was Paignton where we lunched at the popular Dellars Cafe and afterwards enjoyed a walk through the busy streets and on to the beach. These watering places or holiday resorts are made attractive and restful and give facilities for recreation and amusement, and well arranged consideration for the healthy and care for the infirm, and win the hearts of the visitors and the stranger is compelled to feel at home within their gates.

We left here at 2.35 and followed the coast road with its rich and varied coastal sea and landscape view and the steep hills being the gradient of the coast, this was especially so on reaching Brixham Quay. We were pleased to call at this historic fishing place where fishermen were in their usual dress and on the look out sitting or walking to and fro on the quay, with their conversation in Devonshire dialect, may be of the weather, or last nights catch, or the price of herrings or pilchards, but all with a freedom that is equal to their gallantry that is needed in the fisherman's boat.

On the quay a monument is erected to William Prince of Orrange who landed there in the year 1686. The Revd. Gregory Harris has written a poem in the Devonshire dialect in his book "West Country Folk", which gives a charming rendering of the landing and its influence on Brixham people. Our peep at Brixham gave us pleasure, and also an opportunity of motoring through its narrow streets, with houses perched on the hill side and flights of steps to reach them.

We were now on the way to Kingswear and the crossing of the Dart to Dartmouth. It was very interesting going across on the Ferry. We had an experience here, our car was gently propelled to the Ferrybridge platform, but the Lady in charge had omitted to moor the bridge securely consequently with the force and weight of the car the Ferry glided off and our car went axle deep in the river. With great promptitude and presence of mind Mr. George backed the car to safety. The Lady in charge of the slipway was generous with her regrets and tried to convey the thought that her position was of the utmost importance as director of the slipway and collector of the crossing toll. She walked in the water with her Gum knee boots attending to the various duties. The water of the Dart was the element she enjoyed. We all thought Kingswear and Dartmouth two very interesting places viewed from either side of the river Dart. The houses and streets appeared to ascend terrace above terrace to the eminence of its rocky height. All the houses looked as if built to overlook the River, more especially those at Dartmouth.

We had a steep climb from the landing slip to the main street. We left here at 3.40 p.m. our next stop being on Slapton Sands.

This long stretch of beach reminded us of our own Par Beach i.e. in length but the sand itself was of a very course texture. We could not resist the temptation of stopping the car to enjoy a walk or rest on the sands, and to watch the playful waves following each other in merry frolic and spending their energy on the rising beach. At the West end of the beach facilities were available for Teas &c.

We now decided to go on to Plymouth, passing en route, Kingsbridge, Averton, Gifford, Modbury and Yealmpton. We soon had a view of Plymouth, the metropole of the West, now a City with an ancient and chivalrous history, a National stronghold with its Dockyards, Naval and Military Barracks and Air Force Station and holding a unique influence. Probably few families have not had some relative or friend attached to H.M. Dockyards or Naval or Military forces at this Government base. Thus this personal influence of respect toward Plymouth. It has been said that Plymouth is beautifully situated and we must agree that this is so.

As we neared the City, we had on our right the foothills of the wondrous Dartmoor, and on our left the Plymouth Sound, and as we entered the streets we were met by its commercial enterprizes represented by its expansive shops and business warehouses each with their windows attractively displayed.

Time would not permit us to visit the Hoe with its spectacular scope and view of the sea, river and landscape. The Hoe is considered one of the finest promenades in the World. From here we have the English Channel in a wide expansive view and away in the distance the Eddystone Lighthouse, the friend to all sailors, sending forth her light and warning. Nearer the Breakwater, the shelter for the ships maybe of many Nations, the first port of call with many of our Liners, there is also Drake Island, and on the other side of the river is Mount Edgecombe and its famous tropical gardens. As one looks up the Hamoaze one sees battle ships of all classes lying quietly at anchor, and then on the other side Mount Batten with extensive fortifications – an Air Force Station. The beauties of the Hoe appeals to all. Its background is the City and beyond this the Dartmoor, fascinating and impressive. As a dividing line between the hoe and the City there is a line of imposing Hotels and private mansions adding dignity to its out-look. Recreation is provided by its open spaces, Tennis courts and Bowling Green. Its decorated boarders and bed of flowers gives an attraction, flowers having their part in bringing beauty and perfume to all alike. One admires the Drake memorial, the Smeaton Tower and the Great War memorial, which all increase its importance and attraction. If the Hoe could speak no doubt it would talk of its history of Sir Francis Drake and his game of bowls, of Lord Howard of Frobisher, those days (1588) of the Spanish Armada, Yes! the Hoe is a wonderful place and praise should be given to those in Authority.

There are are many features of Historic pleasure if one walks from the Hoe, passing the Citadel Gate with its wonderful architecture and archway opening and thence to the Barbican. Here one passes the busy fishermen and women in the fish market also the crowd of fishing boats and thence on to the May Flower stone. This is the spot where those noble souls for conscience sake left kindred and home, not knowing the perils of sea or the new land they sought. History declares that these Puritan souls were led by an unseen power and protector and further say "What has God wrought'. The Puritan foundation and statesman of qualification, types which stand the test of ages.

In this brief out-line we must not forget the 14th century St. Andrews Church, the Guild Hall, its grand organ its windows and statuory conceived to give the History of the City. Plymouth sent the first Lady M.P. to St. Stephens – Lady Astor – a clever speaker and an ardent worker in the social and temperance course. Plymouth demands these passing thoughts.

We crossed the Ferry at Keyham and entered the Cornish Riviera at Torpoint, and one of the Gates to the West. It has been predicted by eminent authority that cornwall will be Englands future health resort. We decided to stop here for refreshment. The word 'we' could now be used with freedom for we were now in the land of Cornish cousins, and with a freedom of thought that Cornwall was our County and equal in every aspect to any of the Counties we had travelled through.

We left Torpoint at 8 p.m. and stopped at Liskeard for Petrol and the light was now fading. We were now travelling home on pleasant Cornish roads and passing rapidly through Rural and woodland scenery. As we were coming into Tywardreath we had thoughts of thankfulness we had been vouchsafed health and travelling mercies through our 12 days long trail, and we had the joy of knowing that loved ones were waiting for us, for which we had proof as our car stopped at Fairfield. After the pleasant meeting and exchanges of those little kind thoughts and court Mr. George motored us to our 'Little Grey Home in the West', and after a good-night to our friend we joined our own family group and enjoyed the refreshment of food and their warm cheer.

David Grayson expressed himself on his return from the 'Friendly Road" thus:—

> "I discovered that stamped metals are far from
> "being the world's true coin. As a matter of
> "fact there are many things that we prize more
> "highly because they are rarer and more precious".

We proved that friendship is akin to happiness and adds pleasure to life and we can sincerely say this has been our experience.

"Thoughts of Cornwall our beloved County after returning Home!'

Cornwall with its 30 miles (or thereabouts) in length and dwindling width and its 500 miles of rugged and picturesque coast line, bounded by the Atlantic on one side and with the less turbulent English Channel on the South. There are its quaint and sequestered fishing villages and havens almost hid in the valleys by the rocky heights, each village delighting in its own speech and ways, and regarding their boats, nets and gear as the best. A home loving people charged with affection, and their bravery and daring increases with danger. Heroic service either by Life-boat or assisting their mates in time of Gale or danger is only a part of their lifes ambition and their wives are moulded in the same philosophy. Yes, the fisherman braves the Atlantic gale of the sea and loves his fisher home. These men are certainly a source of help to the growing popularity of the Duchy.

Who can speak of the values of the County — its Fish, Tin, and Copper has been added to by its Radium, Clay and other minerals which may yet again survive the bloom in commerce as in the old days.

Its relics of pre-historic history can be traced in the mines, and spotted by cross or stone on the roadside and in our churches. Even the narrow roads are said to be the ways of pre-historic workers conveying the mineral from the mine workings to the creek or loading place, by donkey pannier for far off places. If pre-historic remains are further sought for we have to think of the 7th century church near Perranporth, or the discovery, at Harlyn Bay, of a pre-historic burial ground. Many antiquities have been discovered here and are exhibited in a museum there (Harlyn Bay).

The Cornish Mining industry for seveal decades has gradually declined, the once busy mining district with its music of pumping engine, stamps or water wheel has become silent. There are remains of shafts and workings in the form of burrows and uneven spaces and containing a mineral that even grass refuses to grow upon or cover. These hills of stone and waste burrowed from the depths indicates the danger the miner of the past worked under, and laboured in search of the precious minerals. The condition under which the shaft miner worked was dangerous and also unhealthy, working in water and damp heated atmospheres which often at middle age develops 'Miners Tysis'. The girls and boys often followed their parents occupation, hence the mining industry is bred in their bones. The miner dressed for under ground work wore specially provided hat with a lump of clay on the fore part in which to fix their tallow candle.

With the closing down of the mines the miners imigrated to all parts of the world following the voice of minerals. Hence we hear, there are no mining camps without the Cornish miner or engineer.

If interested in Botany Cornwall's warm and equable air gives to its trees, strength, stature and stability, profuse foliage from the early spring to the late autumn. With the slow decay of leaf it presents pictures of goreous shades which defy copy or an artists reproduction. With this even temperature the Botanist discovered tropical and semi-tropical trees, shrbs and plants flourishing in the open as if in their natural soil; flowers grown in the shelter of our sea side cliffs, often with little soil, or later on the open field or garden produces choice blooms of distinguished colour and rare perfume.

Cornwall with its glorious sunshine playing on its hills and sand dunes its wooded valleys and pleasant lanes, its hospitable and homely villages warmed by the gulf stream and spiced by the moorland air, cooled by the Atlantic breezes. Her coast studded with sandy beaches daily cleaned by the rising and receding tides, spaces where the rich tonic oz`one is pure and healing; safe for bathing, fishinr or sport, with the sea's constant motion of wave as companion and the blue skies as canopy.

The science of music and song are as a true born native of Cornwall, it is the true yearning of the heart fostered by churches and choral societies. In the western part of the County even the ordinary conversation is set to music and conveys a charm only equal to its musical expression. The bands of the County are well organised and are keen for competitions. Bugle is regarded as the centre of Cornwall's popular band contest.

Cornwall has been rich in Saints, the names of places and churches, towns and villages throughout suggest that Cornish people from early history have had regard to relgion and Saintly men. John Wesley came to Cornwall with his message of evangalism founded on principals of salvation by faith and of yielding the heart and life to Christ. His journals state he met with opposition, was refused hospitality and suffered privation and insult. He aroused the County by his energy and depth of purpose, and soon accomplished a great work and quickened the County to their spiritual need. To-day we have chapels and ministeries practically in every town and village and by the wayside.

Who had not read of Dick Hampton and Billy Bray, miner uneducated Evangelists who moved the County in their time by their precaching.

Cornwall has enriched the world with men of culture genius and business acumen, whose names stand prominent in history as Missionaries, Philosphers, Astronomers, Scholars, Artists, Engineers, Inventors and mechanical genius, their discoveries of great and humane principles have lifted England and the world in the scientific scale. Cornwall has still her scholars and learned men. Sir Arthur Quiller-Couch, professor of Literature who Cambridge delights to honour, a stronghold to the education authority of the County and beloved by the people of Foy and author of many books. Cornwall also gave birth to the Revds. Sillas & Joseph Hocking, preachers and authors, who by their writings have claimed recognition for the County. Their popular books are read wherever the English language is spoken. Reference should also be made of the late Revd. Mark Guy Pearcean eminent preacher and Author of reputation.

Cornwall has so many features of interest and delights to welcome its ever growing popularity. Its invigorating air are qualities that restore vigour and over taxed nerves. Its beaches give freedom, its briny waters offer a welcome. Our Country roads offer pleasant surprises and from the hills one has a constant change and new presentations of scenery of the sea and coast with steam or sailing ship on the ocean highway, or of secluded beaches, animated scenes of life and frolic of the visitors and children. Descending the hill, and crossing the granite bridge we have the lovely valley, its quaint village with its unadorned life, the spreading tees giving shade to the roadside and rest and security to the song bird, the music and ripple of the flowing river, and as one traces the valley with its green fields on either side and dotted life of feeding cattle, we smell the perfume of sweet herbs and trace the many shades of wild flowers mindled with their pride and stateliness with the predominent green.

Homes of the birds, butterfiles and insects, suggestive of peace, – rural peace and happiness.

Our thoughts up to the present have been of Cornwall generally, but what of the enchantments of our own district in particular. Let us walk on a summer day from the famous land mark, the Gribben Head, with its beacon warning to mariners. Standing on this head with a southerly breeze clowing, its effect being warm, fresh and bracing, and the ozone as if with a body giving an effect of bouyancy. We say what a facinating view from every point of the compass. We wonder if this boundless view could be eclipsed with its light and shades of the cloud and projecting rock. The sun plays on the great expanse of water and there is interest in tracing the coast line with its constant change of form, of its promotories and rugged cliffs, its bays and inleft. Then there are the Gwinges, standing as a menace to shipping with the bashing white foam and wave shewing the grey rocks and its contour. These rocks are the resting place of the gull and other sea birds, and are situated on the highway of the sea to the clay ports, and calls on the mariner to see his compass and get his true bearings.

Looking across the sea we find the frowning Black head, these two points – Gribben and Black head – form the guardians to the entrance to our rock bound St. Austell Bay. Yes we can safely say beauty all around, if we look to the East we have the picturesque little beach and bay with its Grotto and the scenic beauty of evergreen tall and massive trees and shrubs leading to Menabilly and beyond Fowey.

Continuing our walk to Polkerris, which is formed as a ravine (probably the result or feature of the Ice Age) widening as it nears the sea. Once the home of an extensive fishing industry, and a station of the National Lifeboat Institution, but now only a village of quietude and sylvian beauty. The road leading out of the village is unique being an avenue of tall trees shrubbery and cottage gardens. Its beachis protected from cold winds by its position with high cliffs as a background, its pier to defy the southerly seas and giving ideal life of freedom with its fishing, shrimping and rock climbing facilities.

We climb the steep and winding path to the fields leading to Trill Farm, and rest or linger by the walled gardens, and take from our lunch bastke, Cornish home-made delacies consiting of Cornish pasty, saffron cake, cream jam and pastries also a thermos with tea. No country can provide a more substantial appetising or satisfying meal. We are here confronted with scenery that challenges even imagination to express. We say unique because it baffles description, and with meagre words and limitations we admire the lines of the wide scene before us as of natures conception, decorated by mans invention, need and commercial enterprise. Let us follow the rocky coast line with its beaches. We start from the Black head heights, following the coast to Porthpean beach and village, around the point to the port of Charlestown on the next point the St. Austell Bay Hotel of high appearance and the nucleus of a new town with its inimitable view of sea and coast line, its attractive gardens and the Golf courses, and nestling under rocky protection the Crinnis beach, furnished with tennis courts, refreshment room and attractions for visitors. We have next the Spit beach, one of the growing attractions of our district. It is considered a pretty beach and attractive to Pic-nic parties. Space is given on the field by the County council as a recreation ground with its tea and catering establishment, the place for fun and frolic for the children, and a sun and salt air bath for adults.

At the back of Spit we have the road leading through the Par Moors (once a busy mining centre) to St. Austell. On the right hand side of the road, long clay drys with their white appearance and tall chimneys. These works draw their supplies in a liquid state through pipes from the clay pits, which may be many miles distant. These works are employed for storing and drying the clay. We follow this course with St. Austell's charming hills and sand burrows standing at intervals, bright and sparkling in the sunshine. Then a little nearer we see Par Harbour, interesting because of its trade, with its steam and sailing vessels moored to its long quays, indicating it as a port of importance not only to Par but to the county with its importations of coal, timber, cement and general goods, and extensive shipments of china clay and stone for the trade requirements of the world. It is connected with the main line and gives facilities for the advancing tide of the motor industry. Par is also a good place for boating, fishing and deep sea bathing. As the back ground here we have the once famous Par Consuls Copper and Tin mine, now shorn of active life, a rough and uneven hill with its witness of burrows of stone rubble, crowned with the Mount house, with an undisturbed view of the sea and the coast on the one side and landscape view of equal value and distance on the other. Further to our right we have St. Blazey with its 14th Century church and the Birthplace of Ralf Allen, the reformer of our National postal service. It is also the gateway to Prideaux and the fascinating Luxulyan valley of wondrous beauty, the ideal home of ferns, wildflowers, the bluebell in particular. Its waterfall is both graceful and impressive. Its pleasant walks and picturesque scenery of valley and hill has become known as one of the county's attractions. The moss covered rocks and boulders and overhanging granite suggest upheavals at an early date of its history. The railway line to Newquay runs up the heart of the valley and through a very finely built granite viaduct which also serves the purpose of an aquaduct by carrying a stream of water from the opposite hill. Excursions by motor and rail to this fascinating place gives the public and visitor an ideal change of restfulness presenting a sylvian charm with nature at its best.

      Revd. Gregory Harris in his poem says:-
         "Luxulyn, name of soft seductive sound,
         "Suiting so well this sweet sequestered vale,
         "Deep hid in Cornwall's heart – ...   ...
         "Midst fern and foxglove by the shallow stream,
         "That soothes the senses with its slumberous song,
         "On either side the rock strewn hill sides rise,
         "Bramble and brake in tangled loveliness,
         "Bring Cornwalls charm before her lovers eyes,
         "Making a heaven of wilderness.   ...   ...
         "Luxulyn, once again thy name I breathe,
         "A fleeting tribute to the Queen of Grace,"
         ...   .

Then coming back almost to our feet we see the Par Beach with its long stretch of sand said to be one of the finest expanses of sands in Cornwall. Safe for childrens paddling or bathing, giving the appearance of a long street, with its numerous huts and its crowd of visitors and children gay in bathing costume or sporting with ball or boat. As one notices the voice or expression, we are cognisant with dialects so removed from our own and which have Cockney twang and North country phrases. The Parish Council are to be congratulated in the policy of Beach improvement. Attractions are necessary, amenities are of value and we have now the provision of a model yacht sailing pond, public tennis courts, tea and dance pavilions which are evidently a feature of making Par a popular seaside resort. To the crowd of visitors, Par means a good holiday, a renewal of vigour and a resolve of a return visit. At the back of the beach we have the new seaside villas, looking towards Mount we have also several bungalows, new and up to date. Then there are the beautiful residences and grounds of Penawryn, Scobells and Elmsleigh all being built on disused mines, and as we look towards Par Station a semi-terminus of the Great Western Railway with its branch lines to Newquay and Fowey and then we see Tywardreath stretching out its arm of recently built houses and bungalows towards

Par Station. These homes command an expansive view of the bay and beach.

The many walks of the district lead up the pleasant hill and along roads that may be termed as avenues and lanes, shady and peaceful.

As we return to the Par Beach and scan the field path we have just come along and review its beauty and the 3 miles to the Gribben Head in our hazy imagination, we can picture this Headland as one of Cornwall's health resorts, studded with Hotels and homes, using the advantage of the small picturesque beaches as its base, waiting for exploration and development. At this juncture let us relate a conversation with a gentleman camper, who was asked the question why he selected a spot such as Trill Farm when there were places nearer Par and with more protection from the wind and elements. He replied that he had toured England, Scotland and Wales, but this was the most beautiful spot he knew.

We have not mentioned the exquisite views from Castle Door to Tywardreath. From this elevated hill we look over the next ridge, and have the district of Stenalees and Bugle before us, with their numerous sand dunes apparently reaching the skyline, and the rows of houses, the homes of the clay workers, giving life to the scene. If we linger and look towards Lostwithiel we have a rural picture that claims our attention, intersected with mines, woods, and farm houses. On the left we have Trenython built by Colonel Peard who fought with Garabaldi and was known as Garabaldies Englishman, the late Dr. Gott, Bishop of Truro also resided here. It is now fitted out as a Railway Convalescent home, with accommodation for 80 men. It is situated in a charming position with extensive view and considered one of the best restorative institutions owned by the Railway insurance. We think, too of the hundreds of men that are sent here year by year for recuperation will be a means of advertising our district throughout the United Kingdom.

Tywardreath claims respect as being charmingly situated famous for health and longevity, restful and rich in its residents and their ability as Church and local historians writers & Lecturers. Lanje who writes in our local papers on the historical history of our district claims Tywardreath as his native home.

— : — : — : — : — : — : — : — : —

J. SAINSBURY, GUILDFORD, SURREY.

A LOVELY DAY - IDYLLIC PICNIC

NOTES by the Driver

All the full and excellent description of the places we visited given by
Mr. Parkyn, makes much that I might say, mere redundancy, but a few
notes from the Driver's point of view, might be of some interest. Let me
say at once, that I realised, that I was taking on a responsibility
greater than I had ever done before. I set out with a definite plan to
take my three Passengers practically around much of England, across
and around much of the Scottish Lowlands. No places of the proposed
itinerary was missed, whereas two extras were worked in, via,
Darlington back to Richmond, in Yorkshire, for the eclipse, also around
South Devon, via, Slapton Sands, which, although living in Devonshire
for years, I had never seen before. This brought our total mileage by
Car, to 1.300. Miles (one thousand, three hundred). We used the Car on
ten days, of the twelve we were away. The Thursday and Friday it was
in Garage, at Edinboro', so as to give me a rest from driving. The Car
was a 8 M.P. Fiat, and about 7 months old, and gave us splendid
Service. We had the brakes adjusted at Leicester, and at Edinboro' asked
them to run over the tappetts, but this was done badly, and the
afternoon of the first day, on Homeward Journey, Mr. Parkyn and I
adjusted them ourselves (when in view of Lake Bussenthwaite, a
Glorious stopping place, and what a Tea we had, of local fare) These
were the only adjustments necessary for the trip.

We had a little mishap at Kingswear Ferry. We were guided to the
small Ferry (never again). The ferry was so short that I hesitated to
dash on it, lest I should dash through it. The half speed blow, knocked
the Ferry away, leaving the front of the Car in a foot of salt water,
which made the front brakes screech for many a month.

Habitually driving with care, I specially resolved to excercise
Super care on this trip, and hoped for no trouble, and few punctures
only. As it turned out the only trouble was one puncture, which we
bothered with in the first hour of our journey. Our first day was to be
our longest run for any one day, so I determined to start in good time,
however, it was not to be. I backed my Car out of my Garage, got out to
close door of Garage, but whilst doing this a Milkman brought his horse
and trap, unperceived by me, immediately behind the Car, and the
moment I backed the Car, the shaft of the trap was thrust through the
back of the hood. What an unfortunate start, apart from the delay,
moreso than we knew at the time, as the patch I had to have put on,
was stuck with a kind of dope, which probably brought on the Asthma
attack, which my wife developed two days after, robbing her for days of
the pleasure of the trip. The puncture we had occurred four miles

beyond Lostwithiel. With Mr. Parkyn's help I put on a spare wheel, and had puncture repaired at Liskeard, eventually leaving there about 1o/c. This was the only time we used the spare wheel, which was fortunate, as we had about a Cwt of luggage, piled up on the Grid behind it. It has been said that three troubles usually come together. This we had reason to remember, as that afternoon, passing over the sandy roads of Sedgemoor, a grain of sand got in my eye, it sat quietly until later, when we were in the midst of the Market crowd, in the town of Wells, when it suddenly became active. I at once pulled in to the watertable, and rushed into a Chemists' shop, right on the spot. He with a Camelhair brush THOROUGHLY groomed out my eye. He said "I can't do more" as you will not let me put the brush in. I thought that he must have had the idea of brushing, not the sand, but my eye out, however, I did not say so as he really had done a good job, and the sand was gone. I bought a bottle of lotion, and bathed it. By next day my eye was quite well, and fit for plenty of work. So in the first twenty four hours, all the delays were over.

During the trip, we used to look out for the COUNTY Boundary line, and then noticed any difference in the state of the roads. Most noteable at times. In Oxford county I for the first time saw a man breaking stones by the road side, with a net to keep the flying pieces of stone off the road.

The first day we ran in the following counties :– Cornwall, Devon, Somerset, and Gloucester. Some days we passed through a larger number. First Petrol replacement we had at Okehampton, and then at Templecloud, near Bristol. We entered Bristol just on lighting up time. We rarely went over the same road twice. Once when we doubled back from Darlington, over part of our road to get to Richmond, also Farrington Gurney to Street, and from Liskeard Home. On second we cross a fourturning at Cross Mands, near Chipping Sodbury, going west to East, and on Home journey we crossed again going from North to South, on the way to Bath from Stroud. The roads were new to me, after leaving Wells, excepting Oxford to Banbury, Honiton to Exeter, yet so well were the sheets of our route worked out by the R.A.C., that we only once went out of our way, and then only 1/4 of a mile near THORNE, in Lincolnshire; after leaving EPWORTH.

The only rough roads we encountered were after we entered Scotland, at COLDSTREAM, when we had about fifteen miles of pot hole roads. Our finest views from the Car were :– From, Mingston Downs, Gunnislake, High ground behind Marytavy, Night view of lights from farm at Richmond, in Yorkshire when we saw the lights of Catterick Military Camp, and the miles of roads full of headlights of the hundreds of Cars coming North for the Eclipse. These various roads, looking like long glittering serpents, many miles long,.) The high ground when approaching Scotland, and the finest of all, from the top of Soutra Pass, with the view of the towers and steeples of Edinboro' on our distant Northern skyline, also on way Home. Moors near Crawford, the numerous views in the Lake District, on Moors near Giggleswick, also top of Woodhead (altitude 1.800 feet) both North and Eastern aspects. Again nearing Buxton, and entering Cheltenham, also Painswick, and from plateau North of Bath. These were views which will never be forgotten.

The least pleasant day, from Driver's standpoint, was from Kendal to Glossop, as much of this was on narrow and winding roads. On that afternoon, when pulled right in on left of road, and was putting oil in engine, a Motor Bike with two men on it, dashed towards us from behind, at a furious pace. A Car coming the other way filled remainder of road. The Motor Bike dashed or rather leapt on to the two foot high grass verge between our Car and the left hedge, passing us like a rocket. By a miracle they were not hurt, nor was their machine. We all felt thankful for a fortunate escape. This was a very hot day, but when we got on the top of Woodhead, eighteen hundred feet up, there was quite a gale. We had had good weather most of the time, just a drizzle as we entered Buxton, and heavy rain at Stroud, but we drove right through to fine weather in about one hour.

The fastest piece of road was between EPWORTH and SELBY, and lovely stretch of straight smooth road, were we did ten miles in eighteen minutes, which with four up, a Cwt of luggage, and 8.MP. engine, was good going. The Asthma which my wife had, vanished at Edinboro, so all Members of our party were well on the return journey, and we arrived Home, not the least tired in any way. To me it was most surprising how the Ladies stood the long days, with the long journies without in anyway getting tired. We arrived Home, all feeling the better for our trip, and sorry that such a pleasant holiday had come to an end, yet not really at an end because we are at Home, as I am sure that the memory of it all will be with us, as long as we live.

In conclusion, one word for the FIAT. She did well, and behaved splendidly. No day was too long, no hill or Mountain too steep. The running costs were low, Petrol, oil, tyres, Garaging, parking, cleaning at Edinboro, and small adjustments mentioned, TOTAL one and four fifths penny per mile, less than 1/2d per mile per head. Total mileage 1.300 miles.

ADVERTISING YOUR WARES

HOW WE USED TO SHOP

WHERE TO SHOP FOR YOUR PICNIC -1927

Lucky Dogs!

The season for open air meals is here....and whether Corydon takes Phyllis to Henley in a punt or ruins her wave and complexion in the new sports car....the picnic lunch is a delightful necessity.

The purity and freshness of Sainsbury's wholesome foods is only equalled by the pure and exhilarating air in which you will eat them. With a basketful of picnic dainties from Sainsbury's you can start off with the certain knowledge that you are going to enjoy life's cup to the full, even if it does rain.

This little list contains heaps of good things that are needed by the inner man to make a picnic or a week-end camping holiday a success. Keep it by you as a reminder of the things you will need to pack next Sunday or some other jolly day in the near future.

J. SAINSBURY

Head Depot: Stamford House, Blackfriars, London, S.E.1

PAGE 2

PICNIC PROVENDER

Everything Needed
by

THE INNER MAN

to make a Picnic

or a

Week-End Camping Holiday
an unqualified
success

(*For Prices, see Current List*)

J. SAINSBURY

HEAD OFFICE
STAMFORD HOUSE
BLACKFRIARS
LONDON
S.E.1

57½ Years' Reputation for QUALITY

J. SAINSBURY'S

New Butcher's Shop
4, HIGH STREET,
OXFORD 'PHONE 558.

Deliveries

❖❖❖

DAILY
THROUGHOUT
THE CITY

4th June, 1926.

CAMPING PICNIC

Whether you go for a camping holiday in a caravan or for a cruise in a cabin launch, on no account omit to take with you a supply of preserved vegetables and nourishing soups. On this page we list a few of these easy-to-carry provisions.

SOUPS IN BOTTLES
SELSA Oxtail
    Mock Turtle
    Mulligatawny
BRANDS, Assorted

SOUPS IN TINS
SELSA Oxtail
    Mock Turtle
    Mulligatawny
HEINZ Celery
    Cream of Green Pea
    Tomato
    Spaghetti
BRAND'S, Assorted
SYMINGTON'S, Assorted Packets

ENGLISH VEGETABLES
(In Tins)
(Specially packed for J. Sainsbury)
Stringless Beans
Stringless Beans, sliced
Carrots
Macedoine of Vegetables
Garden Peas

ASPARAGUS, Large Shoots
    " Tips
DELICIOUS TOMATOES
PEAS, Smedley's
    Baxter's
    Chiver's
HEINZ Baked Beans
BAXTER'S Sugar Corn.

Hot soups for cold days ! Iced soup for hot days !
We can suit all kinds of weather.

Only the "Hiker" knows how really delicious food can be

PICNIC DRINKS

When taking hot beverages in a Thermos flask, remember that the flavour of Coffee improves after a few hours in a vacuum flask, whereas tea becomes strong and bitter. It is far better to make tea fresh on the spot selected for the picnic.

COFFEE
ICED
for the Gentlemen

TEA
HOT
for the Ladies.

SUMMER BEVERAGES
Grape Fruit Squash (*Selsa*).   Orange Squash (*Selsa*)
Lemon Squash
Don't forget the water or the Syphon.

PICNIC FRUITS

After the first course of the picnic it is good to open up a can of these delicious fruits which are at their best when purchased from Sainsbury's.

ENGLISH CANNED FRUITS

Blackberries	Gooseberries	Raspberries
Blackcurrants	Greengages	Raspberries and Red
Cherries	Loganberries	Currants
Damsons	Purple Egg	Strawberries
Golden Plums	Plums	Victoria Plums

CANNED FRUITS
CANNED IN THICK SYRUP

Apricots	Pineapple Chunks
Peaches	Pineapple Cubes
Pears	Grape Fruit
Fruit Compote	Green Figs
Pineapple Slices	Mandarin Oranges

Many a picnic has been ruined by forgetting the can opener

Use LESS Water ! Fried Pineapple will give you new zest to withstand the ordeals of the prolonged drought.

TEA TIME PICNIC

For jolly picnic teas you want something more appetising than cakes and bread and butter.....Sainsbury's Potted Meats and Fish, or you may prefer Sardines, Brisling or Salmon.

MEAT & FISH PASTES

Bloater	Prawn	Kipper (Selsa)
Chicken and Ham	Salmon and Anchovy	Patum Peperium
Turkey and Tongue	Salmon and Shrimp	(Gent's Relish)
Lobster	Sardine and Tomato	Sandwich Spread
	Mild Anchovy (Selsa)	

SARDINES
French or Portuguese
Norwegian Brisling
(Sansa)

SALMON
Steaks, Flat Tins, ½'s and 1's.
Tall Tins, 1's.

Place two tins of tall Salmon on the edge of your table cloth to prevent it blowing away

The Sports-car enables you to picnic among the sea breezes

GRANDFATHER PARKYN'S ECLIPSE

A diary written on a journey from Par, Cornwall to Edinburgh in July 1927 taking in the Eclipse in its Totality in Richmond, Yorkshire.

Editor Joy David

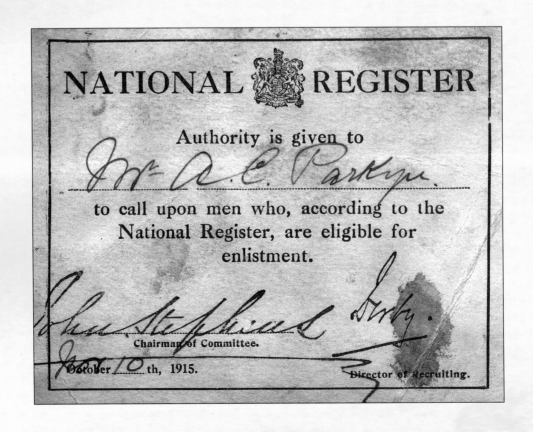

NATIONAL REGISTER

Authority is given to

Mr. A. E. Parkyn.

to call upon men who, according to the National Register, are eligible for enlistment.

Chairman of Committee.

October 10th, 1915.

Director of Recruiting.